America's Be

MW00873887

True Story

An immigrant's story of survival and an opportunity

for a better life

Dr. Bizhan Nasseh

12/7,2020

Dear Mr. Wilson,

You are sport hero of my Grandsons (Nathan, Aaron Barnhart). They thought you and Mrs. Wilson might enjoy reading this heartwarming, humorous, Challenging True story book (my life story).

You are a great player, citizen, and leader, Please enjoy the game, at least 2 more Supperball and MVP are in your future.

Merry Christmas & Happy New Year.

Very Best,

Dr. Bizhan Nasseh

To my Wife, two Daughters, and three Grandchildren

The events in this book are true and recalled from my memory, my notes and pictures, and my wife's input. Many of the people in the book are my friends, colleagues, and enemies. I tried my best to cover their identifications in the capacity that do not change the events. My hope is everybody see the struggle of immigrants to succeed and appreciate how their parents or grandparents as immigrants endured the same journey to survive and build this great country for the future generations to live, serve, love, and share.

Bizhan

PROLOGUE

A retired 73 years old man sits on a bench in a small Park of a city in Puget Sound's shores. His mind travels to times playing bare foot in the dusty cobblestone streets, swimming naked in rough river current, eating forbidden fruits and getting chased by farmers. He recalls daily fights with playmates and kids from other streets and horse carriage rides through barbed wire to show courage. As the first college graduate in his family, he enjoyed competition and coaching sports, playing chess and practicing Karate and Tai Chi. This man had love for education and earned four degrees in the varied subject matter of Criminology, Economics, Computer Science and Education. He wrote computer text book, book chapter for the Columbia University, and published and presented many times in national and international journals and conferences. He gained balance and tranquility though art by painting. Firm military training prepared him for personal and professional challenges and learned to serve with honor. The gift of being husband and father open his heart to love, affection, and responsibility. Managing high security prison, fighting crime and criminals for over 12 years made him to appreciate the value of the social respect, law and order in society. Mystery of his officer and two terrorists' escape from high security prison to Russia created apprehension, agony, and peace after undoing the mystery. Unfair assassination of his young officer by terrorists, chasing and capturing of two terrorists made him appreciate the gift of empathy, forgiveness, and reconciliation. He left a life of luxury in Iran with his wife and daughters, dreaming of a life of stability in the United States of America, with endless opportunity. Believing in the prosperity through education made him and his wife to endure all the challenges offered by their new country. His deportation made him and his family stronger and more appreciative of the opportunities in their new country.

As a university teacher, researcher, and administrator found deep satisfaction and honor in serving, teaching, and sharing knowledge. As husband who is proud of his wife's resilience in raising two daughters while completing her graduate degree and serving university for over 25 years. As father is proud of his daughters' achievement of degrees in Medicine and Law and his talented and hardworking grandchildren, bound to follow in the families' footsteps to serve this great country.

The story is one of heartwarming friendship, drama, survival, love, triumph, and contain humorous recollections of events during first few years in America. The story is about an immigrant, who fought many anonymous battles in his life. The only thing at the end he asks is all try to understand immigrants, their battles in life, their accomplishments, and services to their new country. They are good people with dreams for better life, like your parents and grandparents when they immigrated. Be kind,

understanding, and open minded with them.

Introduction

Leaving Iran

In late 1978, amidst the mounting turmoil of the revolution in Iran, my wife, Bahar, and I made the decision to leave our home in Babol, Iran, for America. Unrest in Iran was steadily increasing as two underground groups with different ideologies, Fadaian Khalgh and Mojahedin Khalgh, revolted against the Shah, the government of Iran, and the Shah's efforts to transform Iran into a westernized country. The false damaging news about Shah's government and promise of a better and fair society for all brought many lower income and middle classes to the opposition's site.

The Fadaian Khalgh, or Sacrifice for People Cause, was the more dangerous and violent of the two groups. This underground group was a follower of communist ideology and Russia. Most of the members of this group were young college students, targeted and brainwashed by Russian publications and propaganda.

The Fadaian Khalgh, which was supported, and armed by the Russian government, destroyed government buildings with explosives and assassinated influential government officials. Their plan was to create fear in society and weaken the Shah's government. By today's standard, they would be identified as terrorists.

The second and considerably less forceful group, Mojahedin Khalgh, or Soldiers of Holy War, was an underground group supported by religious leaders who saw their influences on society evaporate and become limited by the advancement of education, changes in social life, and separation of religion from the government. They were less violent, yet effective in their efforts to penetrate the minds of the young and less educated part of society by arguing that the Shah's futuristic goals were against their religious beliefs.

Destruction was becoming widespread as buildings burned. Fighting in the streets by opposition groups made my job as leader of security force in the city of Babol a hell. My position also made our preparation for leaving Iran a very difficult task. The federal government ordered us—the military and law enforcement officials—not to fight back. Instead, we were expected to negotiate with the opposition groups. Many in the military across the country disagreed with the government's approach to the oppositions. We believed that with permission to use force, we could better control our cities, capture the opposition leaders, and prevent a disastrous, national revolution. The officers in charge in each city knew specifically who fueled the unrest in their locations, and they could easily have terminated the leaders. Frustration and disappointment grew rapidly among the forces, and some were discussing resigning from the force. As a leader, I tried hard to maintain forces' trust and keep morale high by promising that soon the central government would give permission to employ forceful reactions to the unrest. Meanwhile, I grew more concerned about the safety of the businesses and the great people of Babol, as well as for the protection of forces in their daily patrols and services among the violence in the streets. I also feared for my family's safety.

The federal government made a gross, and costly, miscalculation. Securities forces faced increased violence, and leaders in my position were targeted. The escalating tension and widespread violence led to our decision to leave Iran with our young family.

Our last few weeks in Iran were hectic times. Bahar and I had several properties to sell, including our home, which was under construction in Babol; our few acres of orchards near Farahabad, a land between Shahi and Sari; a second home under construction at Shahi; and a lot at Babolsar, on the Caspian Sea shore. We also had to sell our car.

Then came the difficult time for Bahar and I, our four-year-old daughter, Sheila, and younger daughter Shadi, almost two years old, to say goodbye to family and friends, convincing them that our decision to leave Iran for America was the right one. Bahar's mother, and mine, had the most difficult time saying goodbye. A few months earlier, both lost their husbands, and our leaving Iran was too much for them to bear.

On one hand, our families were fearful about our survival in Iran; and on the other hand, they were brokenhearted to see us to leave Iran for an unknown future in America.

We knew that our future in America could be as ambiguous as Iran's future. Bahar and I knew there was a great possibility that we may never again see our beloved mothers, brothers, sisters, and other relatives. Our only hope was for the Shah's government to survive the turmoil, and we could return to Iran ... someday.

Finally, on October 30, 1978, our young family traveled in a rental car from Babol to Tehran, the capital of Iran, about 130 miles away. As we drove through villages and cities, we were stunned by the sight and smell of so many burning buildings, most of which were operated by government, branches of government, or businesses that the opposition believed were owned by Shah's supporters.

We were stopped a few times for investigation by civilians—supporters of the opposition who claimed allegiance to Khomeini, a clergy who was selected as leader of the revolution. I saw the anxiety and apprehension in Bahar's face. I was not sure what would happen if activists recognized me as a captain in Shah's forces.

Usually when we took drives in the car, Sheila and Shadi played and laughed. During this trip, they were very quiet. They were too young to understand, yet they sensed the seriousness of this trip. Anxiety and confusion showed in their young faces.

They could not grasp why we were leaving Iran, why we had said goodbye to family

members, and why some of them had cried. They did not understand why people were

fighting in the streets and buildings were on fire.

I tried to assure myself that we were making the right decision to leave Iran—our

home. To abandon fourteen years of social, financial, and professional accomplishments

and start over in a world so different than the one we knew. My English was limited;

my doubts were not. *Is it possible to start everything fresh, when I am thirty-two and Bahar is*

twenty-seven? Wouldn't we have overcome all of these destructions, if we had orders to act

forcefully from the beginning? I tried to convince myself that, with our resilience, our

experience, and our intelligence, we could make a better future for our daughters and

for ourselves in America. That we had made the right decision. Meanwhile, the events

of last few years such as assassination of young officer by terrorists, chasing and

capturing two terrorists, escape of young officer under my command with two terrorist

from high security prison to Russia, friendship with prisoner who was close associate

with prince and princess of Iran, shooting attempt to kill me, many other stories that I

told in this book were wandering in my mind.

We reached Tehran in the middle of the night. We were saddened to see so much

devastation and destruction in this beautiful city. On streets that were once filled with

thriving businesses and shoppers, small or large groups of angry people with weapons and demolition tools now gathered. The Tehran that we knew was a great, prosperous, peaceful city with happy, courteous, gentle, and generous people. This could not be the same Tehran.

We stayed that night at Bahar's family's home, a small vacation home in northern Tehran. We could hear the chaos and an occasional gunshot in the distance. The children, thankfully, slept, but Bahar and I stayed up all night together, anxious about the Iran's future and our future in the America.

The next morning, my good friend, Captain Hadi Naji, head of a security branch at Mehrabad, Iran's International Airport, and who had also been my roommate for three years at Military Academy, drove us to the airport.

When we arrived, we found that Iran Air was on strike. The strike of Iran Air could be devastating for me and family. We later learned that the Iran Air strike lasted a few months. Fortunately, Hadi checked all airlines and found a few empty seats on Pan American World Airways. He changed our tickets and escorted us to the Pan Am gate. We will always be thankful to my friend Hadi and for the available seats on that flight.

My childhood friend, Javad, who was returning to America with his new wife, Maryam were at Airport and Hadi changed their airline tickets to Pan American Airline. Javad was a doctoral student at Ball State University in Indiana and several months earlier, he helped us to obtain acceptance letters from Ball State—which gave us the opportunity to leave Iran. During the month he was in Iran visiting his family and getting married, the situation in the country rapidly became worse. Bahar and I made the decision then to leave for America with Javad and his new wife. After a few hours of stopover in Rome, our flight continued to New York. Many times, throughout the flight, Bahar and I reviewed our financial, educational, social, and survival plans. All the calculations we made were based on limited knowledge and as much positive thinking as we could muster.

When we landed at JFK Airport in New York on the evening of November 1, 1978, we were informed that our connecting flight to Indianapolis had been cancelled. The airline made new reservations for us for the next morning and paid for our overnight hotel and breakfast in New York. That was our first night in America.

In the last few months in Iran, all faces we saw were bitter and angry. In New York, Bahar and I were surprised to see people smiling and happy. We both felt a great deal of uncertainty but believed this could be a great chance and opportunity for better life in a great country. Every immigrant's early survival tool is believing things somehow would get better. When we arrived at Indianapolis Airport on November 2, Javad rented an Oldsmobile sedan and drove all six of us to Muncie, Indiana — a city with population of 70,000 and home of the Ball State University.

1

Growing with Hope and Ambition

In Iran, people, in general, were born, grew up, worked, lived, and died in the same city. Throughout my childhood, the industrial city of my birth, Shahi — centrally located in Mazandaran (Beautiful State of Caspian Sea) — was home to two nationally known fabric factories, where the majority of its 10,000 residents worked. Shahi was originally called Aliabad, but was renamed in honor of Reza Shah, the Shah of Iran from 1925 to 1941, who was born in a nearby village and was responsible for bringing most of the residents into the city from the State of Azerbaijan to work in the two factories. The rest of the population included people from central Iran; other cities of Mazandaran, which has land and sea borders with Russia; people from Russia; and some natives of the city.

The people from Mazandaran spoke Gilak, in addition to Iran's national language, Farsi. While growing up, I spoke in Gilak with my friends, my mother, my older brother and older sister; however, I spoke Farsi with my father and younger brothers and sisters. My father wanted us to know Farsi to be better prepared for school.

15

My father, David, was born in Amol, a city in northern Mazandaran, and was the oldest son in his family of five boys and two girls. He was a quiet but serious man who loved education and always dressed neatly in a suit and tie. At the age of fourteen, his father recommended that he quit school to start work at a relative's store. My father wanted to continue his education and was not happy with the decision to work at the store. He left Amol and his family at the age of fourteen and moved to Feerouskoh, a small coal-mining town west of Mazandaran, at the middle of Alborz Mountain.

For four years, my father worked at the coal mine and in his free time he completed school. At eighteen, he joined the Army and served for three years. The four years of hard work in the coal mine, followed by three years — two mandatory and one-year voluntary — of rough military services, made him a tough and serious man who badly wanted his children to learn the value of education, to endure challenges, and seize opportunities in life. After three years military service, he was hired by the government to work at the Government's Registration Office in Shahi, where he rented the extra room of a house that belonged to my mother's family.

My mother, Layla, was born and grew up in Shahi, and had two sisters and two brothers. She was beautiful, tireless, and strong mind lady with great love for her seven children. At the age of sixteen, she started working in the fabric factory. The factory was a tough place to work and had an unhealthy environment. The air was constantly filled with thick dust, making breathing very difficult. The scheduled eight-hour shifts changed weekly, from daytime shift to the nighttime shift. Her older brothers and sisters also were working in the fabric factories.

In those days, most of the women wore robes, Chador, which covered the body. Reza Shah, in effort to modernize Iran, started forbidding women to wear Chador in the workplace, and instead forced them to wear European-style clothes and hats. To enforce this rule, police and security forces were authorized to take away the Chador from women even in the middle of the street. In Islam, women must cover the body and hair when they are outside of homes. Religious leaders were against the modernization, which they saw that as a fight against religion. This was the start of the creation of religion opposition groups.

Daily, my father watched my mother in the yard, helping her family prepare food, or leaving home for work in the factory. With long, light brown hair and light-colored eyes, my mother was a beautiful woman. She was also physically strong and could be stubborn. My father fell in love with my mother and my mother also developed deep feeling for him. A year after living in the rented room, my father asked my mother's parents for permission to marry their daughter. After they became married, my mother, who was 17 years old quit working in the factory to stay home and raise a family. It was a great happiness for my father to be part of a larger family, after living on his own for 10 years, since the age of fourteen.

I was born on March 20, 1946, the third of seven children, three girls and four boys. March 20 is the Persian New Year (Noruz). Everybody thought it is a good sign to be born in the New Year, but my father recorded my birth as ten minutes before the Persian New Year (29/12/1324) to be eligible to go school a year sooner. If he recorded it as 1/1/1325, then I would have to wait one more year, when I was seven years old, to start school.

Noruz is the biggest annual celebration in Iran. With thirteen days of national holidays, offices are closed for a week and all schools are closed for two weeks. Every family prepares many kinds of sweets for guests. People wear new clothes, and the young people visit the older friends and family members. The kids receive money as presents from elders. For most families, the new clothes and new shoes are the only ones they will have for the rest of the year, and kids will repair clothes and shoes many times until the next New Year.

For three years after my birth, we lived with my grandparents. Later, our youngest uncle, Saleh, came to live with us just after he completed sixth grade. He had been living in Amol with his older brother's family; however, the family wanted him to start working at a store and not continue his education. My father, even though there were already so many of us, brought Saleh to Shahi so he could continue school while he lived with us. From first day, Saleh became our older brother and a friend for life.

My father always saw the future of Iran as a modern country with separation of religion from the government and the people's daily life. My father did not practice Islam and avoided participation in daily prayers and attending the mosques. He never encouraged his children to practice Islam daily. He was proud of each of us, for our accomplishments in education and in life. He often said to children, "Be the best in education, endure challenge, and seize opportunity when you get one."

My mother practiced Islam on a moderate level; she made her daily prayers at home but did not attend mosque. From childhood, all of us learned from our father and mother how to be tough and withstand challenges without complaining.

Sam's Family Picture

My wife, Bahar, was born and raised in Sari, the beautiful capital city of

Mazandaran, near the Caspian Sea. It is home to all the state departments, which ranks

the city high in social class. Most of the population of about 20,000 people were born

and lived in the area for generations. Sari also has government employees from

different state departments around Iran. The foundation of the city was built during

Reza Shah. Farsi is the main language, but people also speak Gilaki.

Bahar's father, Reza Nasri, was born in Sari and was the only child in his family. His father died before he was born. Reza's father was a wealthy man and owned many homes and many pieces of farmland.

Reza grew up with his mother and was educated in Sari elementary and high schools. Following high school, he served the mandatory two years of service in the military, and then worked in the Department of Justice in Sari. He was the assistant to Mr. Hossain Azimi, and worked at his law firm. There, Reza fell in love with Sedigheh, one of Mr. Azimi's daughters. A year later, they were married. Sedigheh had been an intelligent and bright student, who graduated as valedictorian and went on to work as a math teacher for twenty years. She was a great lady whose vast knowledge and great mind were beyond of the time and description. Her warm smile and calm demeanor made all of us feel happy and gratified.

Reza and Sedigheh had seven children, five of them girls. Bahar was the fourth child in the family. They lived in a large house with many rooms, and a big yard with several different kinds of fruit trees. Reza continued his services in the Justice Department and later was promoted to the head of one of the branches of the Justice Court.

The period of 1960 to 1963 was the key period that saw the Shah's absolute power implemented in the Iranian political and social life. The expansion of the industries created a new group of middle-class workers. The law for political and social equality of women empowered a large population of women, and in 1962, The White Revolution that redistributed lands from big land owners to 2.5 million farmer families created a new and satisfied middle class for Shah. The vision for the changes was to create a massive number of new middle-class supporters for the Shah in Iran. The social, political, and religion changes did not go unopposed by many influential land owners and religious leaders. Some openly criticized the changes, which in some cases, such as the Khomani resistance, ended up with bloodshed. Khomani was a religion teacher at Faziyyeh, a religious school in Qom. Khomani spoke out against changes and White Revolution reform. The government reacted by closing the school, and a few students were killed. Khomani was arrested and exiled to Turkey, and later to Iraq.

The Shah's government's White Revolution was a reason that Bahar's father lost most of the lands that he inherited from his father to the farmers.

Bahar was a beautiful and smart child who was helpful to everybody at home. She was the best student in her K-12 years at school. As a quiet and kind child, her father preferred to take her on many trips with him around the country. Bahar cherishes memories of those trips with her father and often talks about them. Bahar finished high school as top student, and her initial plan was to attend medical school. Fortunately (from my perspective), she changed her mind and attended the Economics College, where she went on to complete her education and meet—and eventually marry—me.

My father, mother, my older sister Mahtob, my newborn brother, Bahman, and I had been living and sleeping in one room at my grandparent's house. I was a curious and hand full three years old. There was a green bean and corn field next to my grandparent's home, separated by a barbed fence. I loved eating the fresh beans, and I sneaked under the barbed fence to the other side to avoid being caught by my parents and the farmer, I hide in the middle of tall branches and ate as much as possible those fresh beans. I also enjoyed playing in a rain-drain on the street in front of the house. On most warm days, I played in the drain and pretended I was swimming, even though most of the time the water was muddy.

When I was three, my father bought an acre of land in the middle of the city and built a new house for us. We were excited to move into our own new house and to have more than one room. The yard was planted with fruit trees—oranges, apples, pears, plums, and peaches. In the middle of the yard was a well, and a pond that was about 8 x10 feet. We all loved to draw the cold, fresh water from the deep well, drink it, and pour it into the pond. Daily, my mother dropped different kind of fresh fruits into the pond to keep them cool and clean for children to eat. After school, the first place we'd head was to the pond to grab a few pieces of fruits to eat. Always, the snack between main meals was fruit, and kids loved those fresh fruits.

Our house had three rooms, each room serving multiple purposes: a large room was for living, and served as my parent's bedroom; in the middle of the house was the dining room, which, at night, was used as the boys' bedroom; and the formal room became the girls' bedroom, as our family grew. We slept on soft, individual mattresses on the ground. Every morning, each kid folded his or her mattress and the cover, stored them in the corner of the room, and opened them when it was time to sleep. My older sister was born two and half years before me; my younger brother was born two years after me; my next sister about two years after him; my youngest sister was born three years after my second sister; and finally, my youngest brother was born three years after my youngest sister.

The greatest advantage of our new home was the location. About 100 yards away was the farmers' market, which had the best fresh fruits and vegetables available, brought daily from nearby villages. Three times a day — morning, noon, and evening — we walked to buy hot breads from one of six different types of bakeries (Nonavaees), which were about 200 yards from our home. The center of the city, shops, a movie theater, and schools were all within a half-mile from our new house.

When we moved to the new place, there were only a few houses on our street, but each house had a few children close to my age. Within a few years, the neighborhood grew rapidly with more houses and more children, which brought playing, fighting, and friendships — all part of the excitement of childhood. About a half-mile to the north were farms, each with a few acres, and a large forest. The nearest farm belonged to a Russian family with a few children, and large milking cows. (People thought the large size cows were brought from America.) As a three-year-old, I was excited to play in a much bigger yard but would also sneak out to the street to watch our neighbors and other children.

Especially in the morning, I liked sneaking out to watch the horses pass our home, hauling loads of fresh fruits, vegetables, and rice to the market. Many younger women also carried goods in large containers over their heads. Their balance while carrying heavy loads, and with such ease, was quite impressive.

At the time, only a few cars were on the roads — mostly American Plymouths and some German Benz. Horse carriage was a popular form of transportation in the city. In order to prevent children from jumping onto the back of carriages for a ride, the backs of the carriages often were covered with barbed wire, which made children's hands and feet bloody when they tried to grab onto the carriage. Some drivers used a long whip to hit the kids who tried to jump on for a ride. Despite the dangers, it was fun and considered courageous to ride in the back of the carriages, and it is something I continued to try, beginning at the age of five. If I came home with injurie on my hands or feet, my parents knew why, and gave me proper punishment.

Most families had many children and preparing two warm meals a day for them required much time. Kids would go on their own to play with friends from morning to evening in summer and after school during the school year. When I was five, I became friends with a group of five- and six-year-old kids in our neighborhood and we played together almost all the time. The street was covered with stones and we played without shoes — no one had gym shoes or proper gym clothes. Our daily games included soccer, running, kite flying, wrestling, hunting, and a game called Tap Choo, which was played with a long stick and a tennis ball. We had only three bases, and would hit the ball, run around the bases, and if the ball reached home base before you got to any base, you were out. Almost every day, during a game or after a game, a fight would break out and a bloody nose was a common sight. If the game was with the kids from a neighboring street, the fight was part of the game.

Most kids knew how to set up traps in the corner of their yards to capture wild birds. I was the only one from my home to know how to set up a wild bird trap. For the trap, I needed the long hairs from a horse tail and flexible sticks. I sneaked behind one of the many horses in the street, and in a fast motion, grabbed one or two hairs from the horse's tail, pulled it fast and escaped away. If a horse's owner captured me, I could receive a hard punishment, and if I was not fast in action, I could get a strong kick from the horse. Once, a horse kicked me before I could get away. The kick hit my left thigh and I could barely walk for a week. In winter, so many wild birds came to the yards, kids had plenty to capture by the traps. My mother was against my hunting. When I hunt or caught a bird, I had to clean it, cook it, and eat it without any help from anybody else.

Another favorite pastime was kite flying. Shops did not have kites to buy, so we made our own kites. We cut old newspaper in the triangle form and cut dried sugarcane branches in thin pieces. We then mixed dried glue with water and made sure not to mess up the floor or yard with glue. Thin pieces of wood were glued to the back of the cut newspaper, vertically and horizontally. We cut narrow, long pieces of newspaper and glued them to make long tails for the kite. We begged Mother for one of her threads to complete the kite project. It was creative, in some cases clumsy, but it worked, and with the wind we flew our homemade kites for hours and enjoyed watching them high in the sky. That was the only time the neighborhood kids were quiet and calm.

From an early age, I was a fast runner and good soccer player. We did not have a designated field and place to play soccer. Kids used public streets in the area, which were only fifteen feet wide, and were dusty with embedded stone. The stones were planted in every few inches in order to reduce muds during rainy days. Our play must be stopped when an adult was walking in the street. If we continued our play and ball touched adult, in the most cases the adult seized our ball and we had to beg and sometimes cried to get the ball back. Our soccer ball was heavy and made with real leather, which made control and shooting difficult. Although we learned how to move and kick the ball to protect our feet from it and the stones planted in the street, it was common for kids to have toe injuries. Even with tall walls on both sides of the street, sometimes our ball ended inside the yard of one of the neighbors, all the houses had 6 to 7 feet walls around them. Getting the ball back required a lot of begging and crying with promises that we would never do it again.

Weekly, the kids from three neighboring streets competed in a cross-country run from Kafsher Colah, a nearby village about two miles away. Each runner represented his street. We walked to the village and from there, about fifteen of us ran to a designated point on a street in the city where other kids were waiting. I was the best runner from our street and should have won most races, but there was a kid three years older than me from the neighboring street who would hit me, or anyone else—hard— who tried to pass him. I always tried to pass him, and he always hurt me, and I ended up in second place. That boy and I saw each other on occasion some years later, when I was an officer and he was a teacher. He apologized about hitting, and we talked about

those events and laughed.

Despite the fun we had, our neighborhood wasn't perfect. Many lower-class

families with financial and law problems were living in our street. Three brothers,

between the ages of twenty and thirty, lived at the end of the street. They were

infamous for fighting with knives and blades, and intimidating rich people for money;

although, sometimes they worked as drivers. They each spent a few months of the year

in prison. They never harmed the neighborhood people, as it was tradition to take care

of neighbors.

Also, in the neighborhood were two brothers who were drug dealers. These two

groups hated each other and frequent fights between those five were part of our

entertainment and curiosity. If they weren't fighting each other, they were fighting

police and detectives who were trying to inspect their homes or trying to arrest them.

Fighting was a common daily event for the kids in the street, by any

disagreement the fight could broke and most of the time ended as wrestling in the

dusty ground. If we did not fight with each other, we often fought with children of

neighboring streets. It was a major problem if a kid from another street passed alone

through a neighboring street. If the boy passing through was caught by the boys of the

other street, he might have been beaten badly. Most of the shops displayed their goods

on a stand in front of the shop. Nuts, sunflower seed, pistachio, and candies were very

29

popular with the kids in the street who were hungry all the time. While the shop keeper inside was busy with customers, kids grabbed a fistful of what was outside and ran away to eat later. Sometimes, shopkeeper and police would chase a boy who had just grabbed a fistful of nuts or candies.

Feeding our large family was a major project. Each morning, my mother bought hot bread and fresh cheese. When we became older, it was my job or Saleh's to buy the fresh baked bread. For breakfast, we drank a glass of tea and ate a piece of bread with cheese. If we were lucky, occasionally we got a small piece of an egg, which was a great treat. For lunch, my mother went back to market, bought meat and other ingredients, and prepared lunch for nine people. We all sat on the floor and each received our share from the meal — we never got more than our share.

My mother's afternoon included a short nap, washing dishes, and then back to market to buy items to prepare for dinner. The food would be different for lunch and dinner. Again, everyone would wash hands, sit on the floor, and receive their share of the meal. The custom was for my father to receive the first share and start eating first. It was a tough job for any mother to practice this routine day after day for years. Fortunately, my mother was a strong and tireless lady with great cooking talent. In those days, there was no oven or range, and most of the cooking was on the open fire or Gas Aladdin.

Those days, babies were born at home and not in hospital. Registering a

birthdate was not very common in the villages, because most areas did not have a

government registry office. Some parents registered their children a few years after

their birth. As I mentioned earlier, my father recorded the time of my birth as before

Noruz so he could send me to school a year early, and I did start school at the age of six

instead of seven. In the class, because of late registering, some kids in my class were

three years older. Wrestling and fighting were common in the schools, and as the

youngest kid in the class, I was a good target for others to challenge. Some days, after

school, I was chased by bigger kids who wanted to fight, and I had to run as fast as I

could from school to home to prevent fighting. Sometimes, I had to fight with much

bigger kids, which resulted in some minor injury.

I was a shy, quiet boy who got along with almost everyone. My younger brother,

Bahman, who is now extremely quiet, was too aggressive back then, and argued with

older kids, mostly with my friends. Older kids started fights with Bahman, giving him

bloody noses. To defend him, I fought with boys bigger than me, and sometimes with

my own friends who were beating Bahman.

Every day, after breakfast, I walked to school, which was about 400 yards from

my home. After morning sessions, we had ninety minutes for lunch. At 11:30, I walked

home, ate lunch then walked back to school by 1:00 p.m. At 3:30, daily school was over,

and I rushed to my street and played until dark or when my mother called me for dinner. From childhood, I enjoyed drawing and math classes. I was good in both subjects and helped classmates and family members with drawing. The drawing was a talent that helped me with teachers and some bully kids. All the teachers had a long stick for punishment of the kids who failed in quizzes, made noises during classes, or did not listen to lecture. For punishment, kids opened the palm of both hands, holding them away from body. The teacher hit both palms several times until kids cried for many minutes. In some cases, teacher slapped by hand to the face and head of the students. I received my shares many times. One time, in fifth grade, my religion teacher was angry that I had not memorized the assigned paragraph from the religion book. He slapped me so hard that I felt on the ground and could not stand up for several minutes; by today's standard, I could have had a concussion.

Teachers were very important in society, were supported unconditionally by parents and schools, kids were supposed to be afraid of them. When kids saw their teachers in the street, they tried to change direction, not to be seen by teachers. Punishment was common and accepted in the schools, and parents always believed the kids had fault and deserved the punishments. When I was in fourth grade, I had a fight with a classmate; his name was Javad. The fight became an opportunity that made us a good friend for life. Javad was kind and loved history, movies, and America. We always talked about America and spent a great deal in each other's houses. Our friendship continued for the next 50 years.

The next few years was more of the same, school, playing in the street, and going to farms to eat fruits, berries, and carrots. Most summer days, after playing soccer or Tap Choo, we sought out fig trees. In my state, the fig trees grew over 20 feet high, with branches spreading outward. Most of the fig trees were on the borders of farms, and farmers did not mind our climbing the trees to take some of the fruits. We moved from one branch to another and picked all the ripe ones to eat. Fig tree leaves, and the fruit, have juice that itches the body badly. After eating figs, we would run to the Tallar River, about a mile away from my home, swam and washed our bodies. The river had strong and dangerous currents, but we knew where the river was deep and safe to swim. We jumped in nude, so we could dry off easily and our parents wouldn't find out we went to the Tallar for swimming. Sometimes, in the absence of a farmer, we sneaked to a cantaloupe or watermelon farm and picked a few to eat them after swimming. If we made miscalculation and the farmer was at his farm, he caught any of us, then a severe punishment could be expected.

A few summers, beginning when I was eight years old, my father sent me by bus to Amol to be with my uncles and cousins. It was about a 30-mile trip on a dusty road in an old and slow bus with full capacity of passengers, and no seats for kids. I had to sit on the floor of the bus, which had many holes. Dust rushed from those holes into the bus and the kids on the floor received a big share of it. When I reached to Amol, one of my uncles and a few cousins were waiting for me at the bus stop. I rushed to my

33

cousin's home, which had a few acres of land full of fruit trees and berries. The house was close to a rough river, which ran through the middle of the city of Amol. The river had wide banks on both sides and about 15 feet lower than the street. The construction companies used the sand and stones in the banks for constructions. The digging of land created many deep pools, some about 50 x 30 feet. We spent hours swimming in these pools and the rest of the time we climbed the trees and picked fruits. Fig trees were everywhere and had plenty of our favored fruits. I was the only one from my family that spent a few weeks of summer in Amol with the relatives.

When I was ten years old, I had a few homing pigeons. I would feed them and fly them from home and street. I also took the pigeons to school and threw them into the air. Pigeons are great navigators and could easily find home from miles away.

I would use my slingshot to hunt wild birds in the forest close to home. I was the only one in the family who hunted, and my mother was against it. She said if you hunt a bird, you cannot waste it. You must clean it, cook it, and eat it. She did not want to do have anything to do with the hunting of wild birds.

Most kids carried slingshots with them all the time for hunting or fighting with other kids. Once, one of the kids shot at me with his slingshot. The small stone hit my head and blood covered my face. I thought my skull was broken. I still have the scar on my head.

The train station and railroad were less than half mile away. Playing in the train station and trying to walk on the rail were another favorite pastime for us kids. It was a great fun and a sign of true courage to stay as close as possible to the train when it was passing at high speed. We also had fun placing a coin on the track, which the train would flatten as it passed over the coin.

Wrestling was the national sport of Iran, with weight lifting and soccer as the next most popular. Our small, tough, blue-collar town produced many national and Olympic champions. When I was ten years old, Imam Ali Habibi, a tall, young man about twenty-three years old, lived on a neighboring street. He won national championship for wrestling, and qualified to try out for the 1956 Melbourne Olympics.

Habibi's main competitor was a wrestler, a physician, who had come in second place at the previous year's world championship. Habibi defeated him twice, but the federation was not convinced Habibi was ready for the Olympics. After many debates and discussions in national newspapers, and public pressure, the wrestling federation was forced to select Habibi.

He went to the Melbourne Olympics, pinned down all his opponents and reached the finals, but he became sick and was hospitalized the night before the final match. The day of the finals he insisted to compete. The coaches allowed it, and he pinned his opponent. He became the Gold Medal Olympic champion and was selected the best wrestler of the Olympics.

Habibi came back a hero and Shah gave him money and a house. All Olympic champions received financial rewards from Shah. Habibi lived in Shahi and won three more world championships, but in the next Olympic Games he lost to an American wrestler. Later, he acted in movies, and became a congressman from our state.

Habibi became an example of what you can accomplish if you dream big and work hard. Because of his accomplishments, many children in Shahi started wrestling, and children wrestling classes were offered for free by coaches at our only gym in Shahi. I was one of those kids who participated in the free lessons. No one had gym clothes, so boys wrestled in their regular clothes for almost six months. The coaches ultimately selected a group of kids who had potential for future training, including me, and asked the selected kids to buy gym clothes, wrestling clothes, and wrestling shoes. I was one of the many of us who could not afford to buy the clothes. I had to stop wrestling.

The two main factories sponsored the city's only gym, which offered many other sports for free to the public. I loved this place and for many years, at every opportunity, I went for soccer practice, or to play table tennis or chess, go for a run, and sometimes to lift weights.

When I was in sixth grade, my father was promoted to the head of the registration office and the government provided us a nice home in the second floor of the building. The building was in the middle of town close to many other government buildings. I was very disappointed that I could not play after school with my friends and could not go to the farms and the forest. I missed my friends, and most of the time I walked to my old neighborhood, which was about half-mile away, to play with them.

Two years after moving to the downtown government building, my father was transferred to head of registration in Noshar, a beautiful city on the Caspian Sea about 80 miles from Shahi. From our home in Noshar, we could see the sea. The next three years, in the summer, I enjoyed every day swimming in the sea from morning to evening. Our school was on the shore next to a large port where Russian ships imported and exported goods. During breaks, students climbed the port's stone walls to watch and to talk with Russian sailors. Even though Noshar was a great vocational city, we all missed Shahi and wished as soon as possible to return to Shahi and live at our home.

In the ninth grade, I was selected to play on the city soccer team, which helped me to become comfortable with a new school and to find new friends. I have three favorite memories of our time in Noshar: 1) It was the only time my father came to my soccer matches — he never came to any of my future competitions; 2) For the region's annual math competition, each school selected three students through internal competition. I placed third in the math competition at my school, and when we competed at the regionals, which included four cities, I placed first. I was the only one with a perfect score of 60 (20 points in each of three math subjects). Everybody was surprised how I placed third in my school, but first in the region. I received the 1st place trophy in a formal reception, and my father was very proud of my achievement in education. And 3) In the three years at Noshar, each summer, my cousins Mohsen, Hossain, and Mostafa came to Noshar, and stayed with us for a few weeks. Our house had multiple rooms, and it was two minutes away from Caspian Sea. Every day after breakfast, we would run to the shore and swim all day, returning home only for a short time for lunch. Saleh, Mohsen, and Hossain were three years older than me, and Mostafa was a year younger than me. We all slept in one room, and in the middle of the night, those three older cousins poured water in Mostafa's bed when he was asleep. In morning, all were waiting quietly to see what Mostafa would do with the wet bed. When he woke up and found himself wet, he assumed he peed during the night. Mostafa quietly took his blanket, went outside, and tried to dry both blanket and his pants before everybody else at home woke up. Those three were dying from laughter but tried hard to keep quiet. They repeated the same thing the next night, and Mostafa believed he peed again during the night. Finally, the third day, I told Mostafa and my mother the story. My mother had a long and tough talk with those three.

There were three types of the high schools in Iran: math, science, and literature. Noshar did not have a math high school so my father sent me back to Shahi to attend the math high school there and live with my older aunt and her son, Mohsen. When I started in tenth grade, Mohsen was already in twelfth grade. We all shared one room for eating and sleeping. My aunt worked in the factory eight hours a day, so Mohsen and I either prepared our food or went to our younger aunt's house to eat there.

My aunt's house was 200 yards from the track and soccer complex. Mohsen and I were there most of the time for practices. He was a great soccer player and goalkeeper. His high school won state and national championship. The same year, he was selected to the state open team, which won the open soccer national championship of Iran. I continued playing soccer in high school. Although I did not take soccer seriously, I was a good athlete — fast, and tall (by Iran's standards) — and dominated my position as right defense.

Shahi was also known for its table tennis team, and our team was the best in the state. Our players were top-tier at the national level. I learned table tennis in a short time and became one of the top table tennis players in my city. In later years, I won twice, College of Economic table tennis championships and competed against other colleges as number one single player.

My preferred sport was Track and Field. Our small, tough, blue-collar town produced many track champions. The most famous, Yazedonpanah, won the national championship in 800 meters many times. During that time —1950s, 1960s and 1970s — Iran's Track and Field was not world class. Iran sent only one or two track and field champions to the Olympic Games, which meant one must be the best of all the champions in various events of the track and field to be selected for this great honor.

Yazedonpanah was selected to represent Iran in the 1960 Rome Olympic Games. For years, I often saw him running in the streets of Shahi toward Sari or running laps around the soccer field. In tenth grade, I had the privilege to learn from this Olympian runner when I became one of his track students. My focus was the 400 meters. Usually, our practices lasted for two hours, which included long warm-up and stretching exercises; over twenty 100-dash runs at full speed; great repetition of the high knee; and ended with a 2-5 kilometer run on the street. Three years, I won our city and regional 400-meters competition, and twice, ranked fourth in State championship.

We ran with flat, cheap gym shoes, and I had only one pair of shoes throughout all the years of practices and competitions. Coach Yazedonpanah was the only one who had cleat running shoes. The biggest gift of my young life until that point was when Coach Yazedonpanah gave me a pair of his older cleat running shoes. Although they were a little small for me, I loved them. I was so proud to show the shoes to everyone,

and when they weren't on my feet, they were tied together by the shoestrings and slung

from my shoulder.

Once or twice a month, after a long practice, if I had a few cents, I stopped by a

bakery close to city center. The owner knew I was coming from practice, and with my

few cents he generously gave me a large glass of warm milk and a big piece of cake. I

could not wait until the next time I had enough money to go back to the bakery for milk

and cake after practice. Those days, kids drank milk only when they were sick. It was

unusual that I had the chance to enjoy a glass of milk as a treat, and not as recovery

from sickness.

My father transferred back to Shahi when I was at the end of eleventh grade, and

my family was so happy to settle back into our old home. It was a pleasure to live there

again and to see old friends and classmates. My math high school was about a mile

outside of the city, and it was fun to run to school in the rain. In the Caspian Sea area,

many of the days were rainy and nobody in the school carried umbrella. Rainy days, we

all came to class soaked and wet.

A few weeks before midterm and final exams, most of the high school students,

including me, studied on the streets after the shops closed at 6:00 or 7:00 p.m., late into

the night. It was common to see many young students seated under a main street's light pole, solving math problems or writing papers. Many students also paced back and forth under the light pole while reading out loud from books to memorize content. Most families had rooms barely enough for sleeping and having many kids sleeping in the same room made it impossible for high school students to have a place at home to study.

During weekends, a few of us went to Mozibagh, a dense forest about a mile from my home. On most days of the summer when school was closed for three months, our gathering place was this forest. We relaxed under the trees, studied, and when tired of studying, we played, ate wild apples, figs, or berries, and chased wild pigs. Some of the kids were skilled in catching snakes by the tail, and then passing them to each other for fun. Shaking snakes while you have the tail prevents them from being able to raise their heads to get close to bite the holder.

Our final exam of the senior year in high school was a national exam. All the students around the country took the exam at the same time, from start to finish, and with all the same questions.

Math majors were required to take tests for ten subjects, most of which were branches of math. In each subject, students could receive scores between 1 and 20. The tests were conducted for five days, two subjects each day. A passing score to graduate math high school was a total of 100 points or more from ten subjects. Students who earned below 100, but more than 70 points, were put on probation and could take the tests again at the end of summer. From the 105 students in my math class, only five of us passed the high school graduation exams at the end of the senior year, and three students were placed on probation status. The remaining students failed and returned the following year to repeat the twelfth grade. Educational achievement was a great honor for family and students. Failing the twelfth grade was a humiliation for student to repeat it and an embarrassment for the family of the failed student.

After graduating from high school, my childhood friend Javad and I wanted to take a long trip during the summer. We decided we'd go visit my older brother, Saleh, who was doing his two years of public military service in a village far away in the Northeast, in the mountains, at the border of Russia. To advance social and health reform and the education of people living in the villages, mountains and deserts of the furthest points of Iran, Shah designed an impressive program that sent young men into those areas to teach children and adults basic health, reading, and writing, instead of doing two years of military service in the Barrack. Saleh was assigned to one of those villages.

Javad and I had enough money to travel by bus to Mashhad, which was 500 miles from Shahi. Saleh told us if we needed anything when we arrived in Mashhad to see a store owner, Haji, who was from the village he was serving. After a day in

Mashhad we went to see Haji in the market, who gave us a few dollars and instruction on how to travel to a village far from Mashhad in mountains. We had enough to eat and sleep on the roof of an old motel. In the summer, for a few cents, some cheap motels would let people sleep on the roof, beneath the open sky on a blanket.

Early the next morning, we traveled five to six hours on an old bus to reach a village between Mashhad and the place where Saleh was serving. The road was dusty through the mountains and the bus was very old. One of the villagers let us stay in their home, where we slept on the floor. The dinner they served was very strange and had an odd smell, but it was custom to eat the dinner the host provided and give thanks, no matter what was served. With great courage, I ate my share of the food, but Javad could not even start his.

We sat on the ground and ate with our hands. I asked for water, and when our host turned away to get the jug, Javad switched our plates. As the host gave me water, Javad said to me, "This food is delicious. You better eat your dinner." With great difficulty, I ate the second plate. I immediately started a plan to repay back his food trick.

We woke up the next morning at 4:00 a.m. to ride on horseback to Saleh's village. When I glanced from the window, I saw there was only one horse and one donkey waiting outside for us. I rushed and got ready before Javad and mounted the horse.

When Javad came out saw the donkey, he was angry at me and was afraid to ride the donkey, but our host assured him it was perfectly safe. The donkey was wild and during our trip through mountains, he took Javad many times to the edge of the cliffs.

Finally, as evening fell, we reached the village. The people were kind, but they had little education and limited knowledge about the society of Iran. Saleh's house had two small rooms; we got one of them. Saleh, from past experiences, knew we might do something to offend the villagers. Saleh cautioned us to take into consideration that the villagers were very old-fashioned and reserved in social customs, including restrictions on talking with young girls. He went over local protocol when villagers invited us into their homes and reminded us to be respectful and kind at all times. We promised to follow his advice and instructions.

The head of village gave Javad and me each a horse to ride, feed, and travel around mountains during our stay. In the hot summer weather, we enjoyed riding to a big pond, which was a great place to swim. In the afternoon many young girls came to the creek that was running in the middle of village to wash the dirty clothes. Javad and I stopped by to watch the girls but did not dare to talk with them. We traveled daily in different directions to discover new scenery and bodies of water to swim in. At night, we could see the strong flash of projectors from the Russian side of the border.

We stayed for a month and enjoyed a simple life in the village with Saleh, who was a generous, and tremendous host. At the end of our visit, Saleh covered our travel expenses to return to Shahi. For many years, Javad and I talked and laughed about this trip and all the events we created or endured.

2

Military Academy,

Learn to Serve with Courage and Honor

In early 1960, Iran had few public and private universities. The few private universities were too expensive for most people, including my family. Public universities were in major cities such as Tehran, Tabriz, Shiraz, and Mashhad. Public universities were free for accepted students, including dorm and meals. Graduated high school students could qualify for public university by passing tough entrance exams. Of those boys and girls graduated from around the country's high schools, only 5%, from throughout the country, were admitted to public universities. The five who graduated from my high school had to compete with the entire country to be included in the small percentage who were accepted to the universities. The remaining 95% high school graduate students who were not accepted to the universities were obligated to perform two years of mandatory military services.

From childhood, my dream was to attend the prestigious Architecture College at University of Tehran; however, the college accepted only fifty students annually, from the entire country. My high school grades were good, but students needed to have excellent grades to be considered for acceptance. I had no chance of being accepted.

Tuition at another private architecture university was $500 annually, which was too much for my family and me to afford.

When I graduated from high school, I was a year younger than my classmates and too young to enter into my mandatory military service. Instead, I continued my preparation for the following year's college entrance exams, focusing on math and physics. I did well in the high school final exams in both math and physics; I changed my focus from architect to these two fields. But instead of my taking the entrance exams in physics and math, my father had other plans for me. He wanted me to attend the military academy in Tehran because it was free, and paid a small monthly allowance for extra expenses. The academy would help me become more focused, and he knew that, as an athlete, I could endure the three years of tough physical requirements and training of the military academy. Also, officers in Shah's military branches were a very important part of society. They had social influence, respect, power, support, and were paid adequately to afford a good life. After a year of preparation to take the national exam for entrance into public university, I, instead, participated in the Military Academy exam. I was disappointed, but I understood the family's financial constraints and my responsibility to follow my father's advice. I also felt more pressure to succeed in Military Academy exam. Without taking the national exams, failure to be accepted by the Military Academy could be devastating for my chance to pursue higher education.

My father and I travelled to Tehran and stayed at a hotel downtown for a few days. The Military Academy acceptance process had two parts to successfully complete. The first was a physical evaluation, which included a 100-meter dash, long jump, pull-ups, and push-ups. From about 6,000 participants, only 2,000, including me, passed the first part and were invited to move on to the second part, the written exams, which were comprised of comprehension, math, writing, and general science. The academy would accept only about 200 to 220 new students, annually. We would not know the results right away.

My father and I returned to Shahi and I felt confident that I would be accepted. The list of accepted applicants was published in the national newspapers, delivered daily by train from Tehran, and every evening, my family, friends, and I checked the newspaper for the acceptance list. Finally, after a month of tough waiting, the list was published in the national newspaper. I was accepted and was the first one from my street and my family who had ever been accepted into college. Acceptance to higher education was a big honor for students, families, and the community, and in our small city, almost everyone knew I had been accepted. They were happy and proud.

The Academy was located in the northern part of Tehran, in Shemran. The area has hot summers and very cold winters. The campus had a beautiful four-story building, a large gym, soccer and track fields, and a cafeteria. On the first level of the building were offices and classrooms; the second level was the dorm for first-year students; and the third and fourth levels were for second- and third-year students. The famous national prison, Zendan Ghaser, was next to the Academy, and once in a while student were sent to assist guards in the general inspections of the prison.

A few weeks after my acceptance into the academy, my father and I travelled to Tehran, stayed a few days in a hotel, prepared and acquired all the initial requirements and necessities from the list given to us by the academy to start my new life as a first-year student.

Military academies around the world are similar in that they have tough mental and physical training programs to prepare officers for the toughest and worst situations. Life in the academy was significantly different for the first-year students, in comparison with the second- and third- year students. The 220 new students were divided into two groups of 110 each, and led by one commander, usually a captain; two lieutenants as assistant officers; and three sergeants selected from top, third-year students. They were in charge of every minute of the life of every student in the academy. Their orders were written in stone and had to be carried out without hesitation.

Father and Sam, start of Academy

Thirty students lived in my dorm. I slept on the top bunk, and a fine young man,

Ebrahim Hadi Naji, slept on the lower one. Hadi and I became close and our friendship

continued after graduation. We each had a tall, standing, metal locker in which to hang

our clothes and store other belongings.

Each of us was also given a heavy stool, which we thought was for sitting. On

the first day of our daily wake-up call, at exactly 5:00 a.m., one of the sergeants stacked

51

a few stools and then kicked them, toppling them over with such an explosive noise that we all jumped from our beds. We were given only a few minutes to clean our area, shave, put on our gear, and then stand in a salute position in front of the beds for check-in. There were enough mirrors in the bathroom for only twenty people at a time, and with only a few minutes to shave, the other hundred had to find a glimpse of their face to shave by moving around or pushing others out of the way.

After check-in by a sergeant, we rushed to line up in front of the building. Each line had nine people, selected by height, and I was the ninth person in the first row, which meant my every mistake could be seen by commanders in the front, and from the side. The lucky ones were those who were short and stayed in the middle of the pack. We sang national and fighting songs while going to cafeteria for breakfast, carrying our stools with us in our left hands. Another use for the heavy stool: to make us stronger. The tables had chairs, but not for first-year students. We were required to hold our stools above our heads while eating breakfast, lunch, or dinner. It took over six months until we had permission for the first time to sit on the stools.

Tehran summers are brutal, averaging 100 degrees and very dry. The first few months, instead of attending classes, we participated in physical activities all day. We each always carried a German rifle, practiced military motions and activities with the heavy rifle, and took it apart and cleaned each piece a few times a day. Our morning run was six miles around the track with rifle in hand, followed by a few hours of field lessons using the rifle in various positions. In any break from military lessons, we ran multiple 100-meter dashes while carrying our rifles. The first three students at the finish line could sit out the next 100-meter run. I almost always came in second or third. (Khatibie, a 400-meter national champion, finished first every time and it was impossible for me to catch him.) To prevent Khatibie and me from finishing in the top three, our commanders sometimes tripped us to the ground, or grabbed our shoulders to slow us down. During military lessons, if anyone made a mistake, all 110 students had to run a few miles and endure tough physical activities.

Lunch was a great break, but short, and the same routine as breakfast—eat while in the standing position, holding our stools above our heads. The few minutes given to eat lunch was not enough time to finish the meal while we were extremely hungry and no meal until dinner time. Some of the students including me hide food in the pocket and ate it when went to after lunch to restroom. After lunch, in the hottest time of the day, strength our heat tolerance, we held our rifles in a salute position and faced the blazing sun while we tried to keep open our eyes. The exhaustion caused many students to faint but not me. With more than twelve years of extensive exercise training from track and field, soccer, and wrestling, I was physically prepared for the academy's tough demands.

Every few weeks, we travelled about twenty miles to a shooting range in the mountainside at the north of Tehran, where we practiced shooting with rifles, handguns, and machine guns. If someone made a careless mistake or did not follow the instructions 100 percent, everyone had to run a few miles up to a designated spot on the mountain and then back down again, a few times.

We participated as a group in daily activities, and if a mistake was made by a first-year student—for example, walking alone in the building—and a second- or third-year student saw him, they could punish the first-year student as much as they wanted, and with any difficult task. I learned this lesson first hand. One day, I walked alone to the restroom, but went to the third floor by mistake — the dorms for second-year students. A few second-year students saw me and were quite happy to have caught a first-year student breaking the rules. They handed me a matchstick and ordered me to use it to measure the hallway. When I completed that task, they took me to the soccer field. It was a rainy day and water was standing on parts of the field. The second-year students ordered me to run laps, and each time they clapped their hands, I had to dive to the field, then stand up and continue running. They repeated this many time until it was not fun for them anymore, then permitted me to go back to my dorm. It was a good lesson — never go near upper-grade students.

After dinner, we continued physical activities, and at 9:00 p.m., we cleaned and prepared our equipment, polished our boots, and prepared clean clothes for the next day. At 10:00 p.m., wearing shirts and shorts, we stood in front of our beds. Our sergeant blew his whistle, and we jumped under our blankets, looking like dead bodies in our beds. Sometimes the sergeant tricked us by calling somebody's name or asking a question. If someone responded to him or made any noise, then we all had to perform pushups, or jump to the bed and back to standing position for 10 to 20 minutes.

In the fall, we began attending daily classes from 9:00 a.m. to 3:00 p.m. Our physical training continued each morning starting 6:00 am, before classes, and resumed directly after classes at 3:00 pm. We studied crime, law, weapons, physical education, strategic and tactical planning, and social issues, with professors who were high-ranking military or civilians from University of Tehran.

Northern Tehran can be very cold in late fall and winter. The early morning physical activities before class each day were performed in very cold weather. The classrooms were warm, and from childhood I loved sleeping. I had difficulty keeping my eyes open and sometimes slept during part of my classes. We were seated in order by our last name. In Farsi, the letter N is almost at the end of the alphabet. I was seated in the last row of a large class. Hadi's last name was Naji, and he was seated next to me.

When commanders looked through windows to check and make sure students were behaving and listening to the professors, Hadi would wake me up, so I would not be in trouble. Between classes, Hadi explained what I missed and what I should study for the next day.

Sam and Hadi, second year Academy

Athletics were very important in the academy. Being on athletic teams was a great advantage and honor; the time spent in practices provided a nice break from the constant military training. All national champions from various sports and soccer players in FC club levels were accepted without entrance exams to the Academy. In every sport, we had top national-level players as students. I tried out for track and was accepted to the 400-meter team. We practiced twice a week from 3:00 p.m. to 6:00 p.m. at Amjadiah, the national soccer and track stadium in Tehran. Khatibie and I rode the bus to the stadium, about three miles away, and walked back. Sometimes at Amjadiah, I saw Yazedonpanah, national champion in 800-meter and my coach in Shahi, practicing with the national team and coaches. Yazedonpanah was kind and made sure I was doing fine in practice and recommended me to third-year student runners to take care of me at the academy.

In addition to track, I was also selected to practice and play with the soccer team. This was a top team and included a national striker, Asghar Sharafi, who later became national assistant coach and then coach. It also featured two top-division one-club players: Reza Moayrian (center back) and Jafar Sharokhi (mid-fielder). They had played at Pas Club, which was in the top two or three soccer FC clubs in Iran, and twice won

Asian Clubs Championship. I played right defense, next to Moayrian. I learned a great

deal from him, and he often praised my effort and good decision-making.

Martial arts and judo were part of physical training, and all students were

required to become efficient in these martial arts. I enjoyed judo, and my experience in

wrestling became helpful in this contact sport. State of Khuzestan had the best boxers at

the national level, and a few of the national team boxers from this state attended the

academy. During our judo classes, they practiced in the boxing ring. When I was a

second-year student, I joined the boxing team and learned a great deal from Safavi, a

student, coach, and national heavyweight champion.

Our academy track team won a regional championship. One morning,

unexpectedly, during the gathering to raise the flag, the general in charge of the

academy called track team members' names, one by one, and handed (the equivalent of)

twenty dollars to each of us as championship awards. As a first-year student, this was a

huge honor. And twenty dollars was a lot of money when considering we had a

monthly allowance of about fifteen dollars. That twenty dollars made my day off very

special (Friday evening until Saturday afternoon). I invited two friends from Shahi to

dinner, drinks, and a movie, all of which cost only six dollars.

Every Friday afternoon at 5:00, we were dismissed from the academy to go home

or go to friends' homes and were required to return by Saturday afternoon at 4:00 —

which meant we had to be back before 3:00 to be ready to line up for the 4:00 check-in at the dorm.

The first two months of the tough training, we lost more than 20 students who resigned, did not return from the day off on Friday, or whose parents came with letters of resignation. The weekend break was an important relief from our grueling daily routines, but it was sad for students who had no one nearby to visit and who had to spend the weekend at the academy. I was one of the few who did not have a place to go on a regular basis. Three childhood friends from Shahi were in Tehran from time to time, and sometimes I would leave and stay overnight with them. Javad, my childhood friend, was one of those friends.

Javad's family had a small vacation home at the south of Tehran, about ten miles from the academy. When he visited Tehran from Shahi, he came to the academy and waited outside for me to be dismissed for the weekend. Then we'd take a few buses to get to his family home, where we enjoyed dinner, drank a little vodka (a popular drink in Iran), and went to a movie.

Javad was an expert in America and American movies. During that time, almost all young people in Iran had dream to go to America for study. From childhood, Javad's dream was to go to America and he prepared to make it happen. By my second year at the Academy, Javad left Iran for Ball State University in Indiana. Javad and I continued our friendship, and in his letters, he explained in detail about his enjoyable student life,

his educational progress, and the great social life on campus and in the city of Muncie,

Indiana. After reading about his new life, I wished I could be there with him. With my

family's expectations and financial status, and my commitment to Military Academy, I

knew it was impossible for me to go to America; but the seed was planted and was

growing in my mind and heart.

With *Javad at Airport, Javad Leaving for America*

After the first six months, we lost about forty students from two divisions. For those of us who had remained, the physical demands of training had made us strong and prepared for any severe condition, which was impossible to imagine when we started as first-year students. We could run for hours in the cold or in the hot sun. We could move all day without stopping to rest and we could climb mountains with our rifle and heavy gear.

The academy gave students two weeks off each summer to go home. Those two weeks were the best times of my life. I received a lot of attention while at home, went to movies and out to eat, and swam in the Caspian Sea with childhood and school friends. The proudest moments came when I wore my flashy student military uniform while being out. In a small city like Shahi, almost everyone knew me from childhood. I received many proud remarks from neighbors, shopkeepers, and people on the streets and became a role model for the younger brothers and sisters. All pursued higher education and graduated from different colleges.

In May 1967, I graduated from the academy as second lieutenant with B.A. in Criminology. In a very elaborate ceremony, Shah awarded all graduates the second lieutenant ranking. At the end of the ceremony, we lined up in a single row, and Shah walked passed us with many generals from three branches of militaries following him. Occasionally, Shah stopped and asked a newly graduated student a few questions. I was one of those lucky ones. He asked where I was from and what I wanted to do. When I answered that I was from Shahi — the city named after his father — he smiled and said he was happy to hear that.

The academy selected three volunteers to train to become fighter jet pilots. They would be sent to Texas for three years of training. Seven volunteers, including me, indicated interest for this three year training. Shortly thereafter, I went to Shahi for a few days of vacation. My mother was very upset about my plan to become a fighter jet pilot and leave three years. She said I needed to come back to Shahi and stay close by to help my brothers and sisters with their education and life. I withdrew my name from the list. In the long run, it turned out to be a great decision to be nearby to help with the family.

Picture with Shah

3

State Prison,

Toughness has Real Meaning

Following the graduation ceremony, we assembled in the academy auditorium. It was time to receive our assignments to the twelve States in Iran. Everyone's wish was to be assigned to his home state. With four others, I was assigned to my state, the State of Mazandaran. One evening in the street of Shahi, I saw Amir the young gymnastic champion and his brother Hamid. Amir told me, after consultation with family and evaluation of his two choices of colleges, he made decision to go to military academy and appreciated my input. I congratulated him and wished him great success in the Academy.

A week after graduation, the five graduated officers who were assigned to State of Mazandaran, gathered at the General's office in Sari, the state capital, to learn where they would be transferred. My wish was to be assigned to Ethelahat, the equivalent of CIA. I was the tallest and most athletic in the group of five young officers. After studying our back ground and asking a few questions, the General told us "Dismissed, back in 15 minutes for the decisions." The five of us nervously waited outside of his office for 15 minutes. We knew one officer needed for the state prison, which was the worst possible job for the new graduated officer. Five of us wished not to be the one for this job. When we returned to general's office, he called my name first and said, "I assigned you to the state prison and you will start tomorrow morning at 8:00, he continued, Dismiss." I replied "Yes, Sir" left the room.

The current state prison was an old one with multiple buildings. It was such a bad shape that some of the prisoners were sleeping in tents at the yard of the prison. State was in the process of building a new prison located outside the city of Sari, which was scheduled to be completed the following year. Meanwhile, the plan was to move all the prisoners, temporarily, to a larger prison in Babol, a city twenty miles from Sari.

There were more than 1,200 prisoners from around the country incarcerated in the old prison building: around one hundred murderers; fifty political prisoners, some of whom were terrorists and dangerous; many thieves; and more than fifty women (a few were murderers among them). Another ten or so prisoners were sentenced to execution.

In state and federal prisons, convicts create many levels of hierarchy inside for controlling the markets, drugs, and power. They are generally divided into groups, and each of these groups has one leader. One group sells goods inside for any price they can get. Another distributes drug and medicines. The toughest few prisoners make up the "intimidator group" that bullies other groups to receiving a share from them, and collects money from rich prisoners by protection them from others.

Our prison had 140 officers in service, divided into two groups. Each was on duty 24 hours, then rested 24 hours. I was commander of one of the groups, and an experienced first lieutenant officer commanded the other. During my first night of service, a few in the top of the prisoner hierarchy planned to test or scare me. What they did not know I was from a tough working city of Shahi and learned to deal with conflicts and fighting from childhood. In addition, I was a good athlete who knew judo and boxing.

Two murderers arranged a faked fight and made each other bloody. All guards under my command were interested to see how I would handle this unexpected situation. I brought the two prisoners to my office, and after investigation, determined one was guilty. The convict screamed at me and jumped forward to grab me, but before he reached me, I punched a straight right to his face. The blow gave him a cut, and blood covered his face. Guards stood by and watched, and none moved in to help. He then tried to grab a chair and I hit him with a left hook that dropped him to the ground. Once they saw enough of what I was capable of, the guards rushed in and handcuffed him.

I knew that if I did not react strongly, I would have a tough time during my shift in controlling over 1,000 prisoners. So, I hanged the prisoner by his hands on the high metal net surrounding the perimeter of the prison, where the others could see him. After a few hours of pain from hanging there, he apologized and requested forgiveness. He was a murderer from the neighboring State of Mashhad, and everyone was afraid of him. I released him and explained that in no way would I be intimidated by him, or by any other leaders at the prison. I told him to tell the others that if anyone made a mistake during my 24 hours on duty, they would have tough consequences. The next morning, the captain who was head of the prison came told me he had heard the news and that my actions were against the law, but he had loved my punishment technique, nonetheless.

Courts, judges, and prosecutors were supportive of officers in charge of prisons and generally disregarded any claim against officers that reached them. They knew that, in Iran, prisons were tough, dangerous, and the conditions made it extremely difficult to control and execute rules and daily functions without force. Criminals filed complaints and claims were not well-received by courts. Most complaints were from murderers and extremely dangerous prisoners who were awaiting execution or serving life in prison, who were unwilling to cooperate with the daily routines. The lower-level criminals quietly endured their sentences and focused on their release day from prison.

Every day at a defined time, for two hours, all prisoners went to an open area outdoors for fresh air, and those two hours gave us the opportunity to investigate cells for drugs or weapons, such as knifes and broken glass. The leaders of the prisoner groups usually ignored the rules for going outdoors, and their actions had been tolerated before by guards in order to keep the prison environment calm. Not during my 24-hour shift. I ordered *all* prisoners to go out — with no exceptions. To help prevent conflict and unrest in the prison, many of the guards under my command asked me to please allow the disorderly group leaders to stay inside. I pressed on with my "no exceptions" rule that all had to go outside, which sometimes led to conflicts with prisoners who were leaders of the groups in the prison. Dealing with criminals is the toughest job in the world, and all authorities knew the difficulties of day by day operations in the prison, and unconditionally supported officers in the charge of prison. We had the system to implement any punishments that we thought could be effective to control prisoners and to execute daily programs in the prison.

Fighting and stabbings to intimidate other groups or individuals was common practice in prison. To diminish such fighting during my shift, I established a zero-tolerance policy to be met with strong punishments. My stand against all these wrongdoings made me well-known in the regional prisons and became my base for

many future conflicts between me and prison group leaders for years to come.

To execute daily programs, I punished any prisoner, even leaders, who did not

obey. In addition to punishment, I shifted some of the advantages, such as selling goods

from leaders, troublemakers, and dangerous prisoners to the other groups of long-term

prisoners who obeyed regulations and were kind to other prisoners. It was authority of

the officers in charge of the prison to award to prisoners or take away from them the

compensations such as selling goods or cleaning inside of the prison.

My strong stand to execute rules and punishments created negative and

dangerous reactions against me by prisoners. I was attacked with broken glass, nails,

and boiled water. I had a few informants in the prison, who had warned me about plans

made against me, and in each case, I made sure those attackers paid a heavy price in

order to prevent and to limit their future plans.

One of the most dangerous prisoners was known in the region was OZ. He was a

large man who had killed three people and had been sentenced to life in prison. He was

a man all other group leader paid ransom to in order to keep him on their side. He was

a known prisoner in the state and any attempt to transfer him to another prison was

rejected strongly by a receiving prison. OZ was serving time at the Babol's prison when

all the prisoners from Sari's old prison were moved there. I was a few months in service at the time, and the head of Babol's force was a tough colonel who came from federal prison in Tehran. He knew about OZ and ordered all of us to ignore OZ as much as possible.

OZ heard about my zero-tolerance policy and tough punishments, and he wanted to prove that he could get away with any wrongdoing during my shift. One evening during my first week at Babol, I heard loud noises from inside and screams for help. I sent a few guards to investigate. They reported back that OZ had injured, with a nail, a few prisoners who had disobeyed his orders to pay him a share from profits gained from selling snacks and cigarettes. I sent a few more guards to bring OZ to my office. The guards reported that OZ refused to come, and he have them a message for me: "If the lieutenant wants me, he must come to get me."

From my first day at Babol's prison, I expected such a situation would happen. I knew that if I lost this battle, I would lose the control of the prison to OZ and his group. I took off my uniform jacket and hat, bent my shoes (in those days, intimidators and fighters wore shoes with the back of the shoe under heels, then dragged the shoes on the ground to make noise). I sent a few guards ahead to inform him that I was coming. The guards were from Sari's prison, knew I wanted to fight and tried hard to convince me not to go. I took two guards with me to OZ's cell. Each cell housed ten prisoners. I ordered the other prisoners in OZ's cell to leave. OZ knew I came for a fight, and he

thought this was his chance to take over the inside of the prison.

Almost everyone, including guards and prisoners, knew that I was a boxer while

in the Military Academy. Upon my arrival at Babol, I practiced with Babol's boxing

team three times a week at the city gym. OZ was about 6-foot-one and about 220

pounds. I was 6 feet tall and 165 pounds, but I was sure he was aware of my boxing

background and my hope was he might come to his senses and not initiate a fight with

me.

I ordered him follow me to the office. He refused and laughed. In order to make

my action 100 percent legal and accepted by my boss, the public, and the court, I knew I

had to force OZ to initiate the fight. I poked at his chest with my fingers and ordered

him to follow me to the front office. He laughed louder and told me that I was wasting

my time. The eyes of murderers and violent people can tell a lot about their intentions.

When they are angry, their eyes rapidly move side to side, and at the time of attack,

their eyes will narrow until almost closed. I carefully watched OZ's eyes. They were

moving rapidly, and knew with one more push, he would attack. I pushed him again in

the chest with my fingers and ordered him to follow me to the office, then I took one

step back to create space.

The second push gave the reaction I expected. OZ threw two punches, but it was easy for me to take another half-step back, beyond his reach. I came forward one step with strong left and right punches to his upper nose and around his eyes. The punches blinded him for a short time and he lost his balance. Guards rushed to handcuff him and dragged him to an individual cell. An individual cell is too small to stretch out for sleeping, has no light, and is isolated from the rest of the prison population. I added some cold water on the floor of the cell to prevent him from sitting. All the prisoners were glad to see this happen and were hoping he'd be confined there for at least for a few weeks to keep protected from his wrath.

The next morning, when the colonel received the news, I was summoned to his office. He said my actions were illegal, but that OZ deserved the punishment, and he supported my actions. OZ's individual cell's floor was dried from the last night water and he was confined there for two weeks.

The punishment news spread to other prisons in the state and to the public in the city of Babol. I received a phone call of appreciation from the father of one of the young men OZ had killed. Other prison officials and courts heard the news, and were happy appreciated how I dealt with OZ.

For the next five years of my services in the prison, OZ and I had many conflicts, and although I had the upper hand in each event, he continued his resistance with new methods, encouraging other prisoners to join his cause. We once had about fifty political terrorist prisoners. We had orders from the federal government to treat the political prisoners with kindness, thinking our extra efforts to help them in prison might change their minds about the government and Shah once they were released. The political prisoners knew they would be treated much differently from the other prisoners, and some tried taking advantage of that.

OZ became friends with one such political prisoner, the young son of a religious leader. OZ's calculation was that I could not touch the son of the religious leader, even if he tried to harm me. He and the young prisoner planned to splash boiling water on my face while I made my daily inspection of the inside the prison. One of the informants warned me, but no one knew when and where it was going to happen. To try to convince me there was no plan to harm me, the young political prisoner often carried a kettle of water for making tea while I was making inspection rounds inside of prison.

Finally, one day when I was inside, he walked toward me with a kettle of hot water, while at the same time, two prisoners pushed each other and made loud noises on the other side of the prison to distract me. I was lucky to anticipate this might be when he planned to execute his attack. He jumped to grab me and raised the kettle to pour hot water on my face. When his hand went up, I punched a straight right to his chin and pushed him back. He lost his balance, fell to the ground, and the boiling water burned his hand.

For five years, the challenge of running the prison the way I thought was fair became a difficult part of my job and my life. The negative psychological and mental effects of dealing with murderers and criminals are detrimental and destructive. Fortunately, having demanding parents, strong believe in greater future, and growing in tough neighborhood and military academy helped me to endure the harsh six years services in the prison without lifelong negative effect. Running a prison with more than 1,000 prisoners might be the toughest mental and psychological job in the world. Regular exercise would be one of the best ways to reduce the tension and stress. I always enjoyed serious exercise and Babol had a beautiful public gym, which was a perfect place for me to exercise. Boxing was my first choice and Babol had a good tradition in boxing.

A few state and national champion boxers came from Babol and boxing was very serious sport in this city. After we moved the prisoners to city of Babol, I joined the boxing team of the city of Babol for the evening practices in the city gym. After a few months practicing with the boxing team, I was asked to be coach of the boxing team of the Babol and later the coach of the state boxing team. Jamshid Pakmanish, the national champion at the time, who was from Babol and member of the city boxing team did not have a good sparring partner, and I was asked to practice and spar almost every training session with him. The sparring with Jamshid who was heavier than me and an excellent boxer made me stronger and much better boxer.

For the next few years, I continued coaching the state team and took them to the national championships in Mashhad, where I received my coaching certification by participating in four days of classes conducted by the head coach of the Bulgarian boxing team. In the national championship in Ahvaz a year later, I was tested and received the first-degree boxing referee and judge certification from Iran Boxing Federation. Our team won two individual national titles and a few third places. As part of training, every Friday, we ran 10k, then went to the public baths and ate lunch together. For the next four years, I continued my contributions to advance boxing in the state. I raised funds for better boxing equipment and a new state-of-the-art boxing ring for the Babol boxing team. Jamshid and I continued our friendship, and he frequently visited my home over the years.

All this time, I still lived with my parents in Shahi, and daily traveled to Babol. All my childhood friends had left Shahi to other cities or to the outside of Iran. Babol was a rich and beautiful city and I enjoyed spending my free time there with new friends, a few businessmen and a few officers.

The prison was in the heart of the city, which made it easy to walk to the gym and restaurants, and to go to friends' stores. In Iran, usually, people who work in government offices had free afternoon, would spend a great deal of afternoon free times at the friends' stores, drinking tea and talking while the store owner served customers. Some of the late evenings of my free days, I walked back to the prison and slept in the officer's room or stayed in my cousin's home in Babol instead of returning to Shahi.

Pictures of State Boxing at national championships

4

Bahman Hojat, Royal Prisoner

During my second year of the service at Babol Prison, the colonel called the three officers in charge of the prison to his office. "Tomorrow, we are going to receive a special prisoner from Tehran" colonel said. "Yes sir" officers replied. "The prisoner is from General Hojat's family, a close family friend of the Shah's family," colonel continued. "Sir, what is his name and his crime?" I asked. Colonel replied, "His name is Bahman Hojat, and his crime is not mentioned in the transfer letter." "You are going to be placed him in one of the guards' room, not inside of the prison." colonel said with emphasized and louder voice. He continued, "Bahman is close friend of Princess Shanaz, Shah's daughter, and Prince Ali, Shah's nephew." Colonel emphasized to three of us "Respect his privacy and as much as possible and make it easy and comfortable for him in the prison." "Do you have any question?" colonel asked. "No, Sir" three officers replied in the salute positions. Before leaving the room, one of the officers asked "Sir, does he wear his own cloth or prisoner one?", "No his own cloths and will keep all his stuffs." colonel said and continued with strong voice. "Make sure ask me first before any action you need to take about this prisoner, I am telling to all three of you." colonel said. "Yes, sir will do" officers replied.

We prepared one of the guard's rooms outside of the main cells for Bahman. When he arrived, he was accompanied by two special guards, and was without handcuffs. Bahman was a handsome young man, twenty-six years old, about five-foot-ten and 160 pounds, with light hair and blue eyes. He was calm, quiet, smart, and very knowledgeable about Iran's government, social and political issues around the world. Within a week, he learned almost everything about our prison, the prisoners, officers, and guards.

Bahman hated the bully prisoners and appreciated that I did not tolerate their wrong doing, yet fair, in how I managed the prison and guards. We became good friends and during my free time, I sat in his room and we listened to Beatles songs from records that he had brought from England.

On Bahman's first night in Babol prison, I received a special telephone call from Shah's castle in Tehran. It was from Princess Shanaz. She introduced herself and asked politely to speak with Bahman. I brought Bahman to my office and they talked for about half an hour about their trips around Europe and what they'd do when Bahman became free.

Once or twice a week, I received a call from Princess Shanaz for Bahman, as well as from Prince Ali, Cathy Adle, daughter of Dr. Adle, who was the head of the political

78

system in Iran and Shah's doctor and best friend. These and other well-known people and national figures, such as the Secretary of Urban and Planning, came from Tehran to visit Bahman mostly during my shifts.

Bahman explained why he had been imprisoned. He had reservations and objections with some of the Shah's policies, and discussed his views openly with his above friends, mainly the children of influential people, and others. Bahman was the leader of this group, and they traveled together, enjoying a fun and lavish lifestyle, which involved alcohol and sometimes drugs. Their parents tried a few times to break up the friendships in order to prevent national embarrassment by their wrongdoing around the world. Finally, they decided the most effective way to disband this group of friends was to separate Bahman from the others by sending him to prison for a year.

Bahman loved to read, listen to music, and drink tea. He was a tough-minded individual, and at the same time extremely kind to those less fortunate. He often helped prisoners who needed financial or medical help. His wish was to someday create a community where people worked, shared, and lived together in harmony.

Shah forgave Bahman and reduced his sentence from a year to six months. On Bahman's first day of freedom, his close friends came from Tehran to Babol and escorted him back to Tehran. He gave his Beatles records and a few of his books to me in appreciation and gave the rest of his belongings to prisoners.

For the next two weeks, Bahman called every other day from Tehran. We talked about prison, his and my future, and what the group was planning to do next. After a month, Bahman came to Babol, driving a Chevrolet Corvette, and asked me to go Tehran with him. I did, and we stayed at a beautiful house at the top of mountain, North of Tehran. The home belonged to Cathy Adle. She was a beautiful lady with long hair and light-colored eyes. A few years' earlier Cathy legs were paralyzed from an accident while mountain climbing with Prince Ali in the North of Tehran. Bahman and Cathy were planning to marry soon.

On my second trip to Tehran, Bahman asked "Why would not you move to Tehran, Sam?" He continued: "You can pick any job you wish, perhaps as one of the Shah's guard." I said: "Thanks for suggestion." Sam continued: "I love your special opportunity, but I have a responsibility to oversee my five younger brothers and sisters." Bahman: "We will talk again soon about your move to Tehran." "Thanks." Sam replied. A few weeks later, I received a phone call from the wife of the head of Savak (intelligence agency, like CIA), who said that I had been recommended by Bahman and his royal friends. She asked me to choose any job I wished in Iran. I told her that appreciated the offer but gave the same reason for staying in my current position. In later years, Bahman would be a great help to my relatives and friends for getting good, high-paying jobs in private and government organizations.

A year after his release, Bahman and Cathy married and bought a few hundred acres of farmland in a village about 100 miles south of Tehran. Here, they built dozens of small houses for people wanted to be part of farming and sharing together program. They farmed what they needed for their families, and shared, but not sold, their products. Bahman and Cathy's idea was to work together, plant together, share together, eat together, and live together. The farm and houses belonged to the people who were working on the farm, with equal shares. We continued once a while our phone conversations. In 1972, when Bahar and I married, Bahman could not make it to our wedding, but send an amount of money as wedding gift that was a great financial help.

Years later, after Bahar and I met and were married, Bahman asked Bahar and I to visit them on the farm. Bahar and I drove over 200 miles from Babol to Tehran, then Tehran to the village. When we arrived, Cathy told us Bahman had to go to Tehran, and asked us to stay a few days. The farm was big, well designed and well planted. Their house was not much larger than the farmers' houses. Their house had a few bedrooms and was built at the far end of the farm with about ten smaller houses for farmers and their families in the short distance. Bahar and I enjoyed our visit with Cathy and their beautiful one-year-old daughter.

The last time I saw Bahman was a year later. Bahar, and I and our daughter, Sheila, who was only a few months old, were at home one evening when someone knocked on our door. Bahar opened the door and there stood Bahman and Prince Ali, Shah's nephew. We were surprised and happy to see them. We talked most of the night, they played with Sheila, and Bahar made a nice dinner, which they enjoyed and asked to take the rest with them in the morning. They left the next morning for Gorgon, a city about 50 miles east of the Sari to visit friends and to go hunting.

I did not see Bahman for the next few years, but once a while we enjoyed a long telephone conversation.

Picture with Bahman at Babol Prison

After spending more than twenty months in our temporary facility in Babol, our new seven-acre prison at Sari was ready for us. The prisoners were moved to the new, more secure prison located outside of Sari. It took a few weeks to move all the prisoners from Babol.

Twenty-foot tall cement walls surrounded the prison yard, and guards with machine guns were posted at four towers. The massive building had strong walls, which made even the best escape tools useless. A long hallway inside the building held locked, smaller hallways on either side. Each smaller hallway had many cells on both sides, and each cell had several rooms, with walls on three sides and bars on the hallway side. Each room held at least ten prisoners.

Prisoners were assigned to the cells based on the severity of their crimes, conviction and sentencing. Rest areas for officers and guards were attached to the main building, and a woodworking factory was next to the building. Working in the factory was a great privilege, and not only helped the prisoners to endure the time, but also paid them a portion of their products' profits. The prisoners were selected based on their skills and attitude in the prison. The prisoners made all different kinds of furniture to sell. Most of the furniture was purchased by the officers and guards and the rest was sold in the market.

The five officers in charge of the prison modified and developed some new procedures and programs for daily operations in this huge new environment. Two younger officers each had 24-hour shifts with about 70 guards in each shift, and the three head officers, including me, worked daily from 7:30 am to 1:30 pm. Sometimes the three head officers unexpectedly stopped by and spent a few hours with the younger officer in charge of the guards and daily operations.

Before end of the first year in the new Sari prison, two just graduated young officers were transferred to the prison. They replaced our two officers who were in charge of the 24 hours daily shifts. One of the young officers was Amir Hossain Ahmadian, whom I had known since I was in high school and asked my advice for college selection when I was third year in academy. At the prison, Amir worked closely with me and report to me. He was tough, direct, and fair with prisoners. His personality and approach matched mine and we became close friends. Frequently, we went swimming in the Caspian Sea, ate dinner together, and went to movies. He knew my family and I knew his.

Prisoners consider it a big honor to be selected by an officer to help with his daily needs, such as cleaning his office, rest area, and shower, and delivering his food. In addition to receiving extra money as an officer's helper, the prisoner could go anywhere inside the prison, eat the best food, and was respected by other prisoners.

Usually, officers select a temporary prisoner with a non-violent conviction as a helper. Officer Ahmadian selected a red-haired murderer from Northern Mazandaran as our helper — which shows what type of person Amir was. Everyone, including other officers and family members, objected to his choice. They joked that someday the helper would kill both Amir and me while we slept.

Amir and I were athletic. For exercise, we ran laps around the prison for an hour a few times a week. We always talked about life, sports, family, and politics. Amir was angry with Shah's government, how his father had been working in the tough environment of the fabric factory, six or seven days a week, for the thirty-five years, yet still struggled with necessities for a good life. I was worried that consequence of his dissatisfaction with officials and government would affect his daily work and future. I encouraged Amir to help his family as much as possible, and to focus on his bright professional, social, and financial future. Many times, I met with Amir's family. They appreciated my positive influences on him.

5

Great Fortune,

Marrying Bahar

In Iran, to have multiple degrees or a graduate degree was a big honor and could create opportunities for advancement in work and life. Having multiple or higher degrees in the military could facilitate advancement as a higher-ranking officer. With the hope of someday being considered for the highest ranking of general, I continued my academic studies towards a second degree.

There was a College of Economics in the city of Babolsar, beautiful small town at the shore of the Caspian Sea. In the summer of 1970, my younger sister, Nazenin, registered for the entrance exam, which was to be taken in Tehran. My father asked me to go with her. I decided to also register and take the exam. After a few weeks, the national newspaper announced the 400 accepted students out of the 3,000 applicants. My sister and I both were accepted.

At that time, I had just been promoted to first lieutenant at the Sari Prison. Daily, two buses took about sixty students from Sari to the college at Babolsar, about 35 miles away. The buses left for Babolsar at 1:30 p.m. and returned to Sari at 7:30 p.m. In Iran, most government offices and military branches open daily from 7:30 a.m. to 1:30 p.m.

If you haven't lived it, it's hard to understand how mentally and emotionally challenging it can be to work and live everyday with more than 1,000 prisoners. Being a student again, and as an officer, brought new appreciation for education—sitting in the

classroom, sharing thoughts and time with younger students from around the country,

and enjoying being in an environment

exactly opposite of what I had at the prison.

Bahar and Sam at College

A few nice-looking young ladies were among the students from Sari, but one

was, by far, the best — not only was she breathtakingly beautiful, she also had a

graceful personality and impeccable complexion that separated her from all other girls.

She had an angel face with long, striking, dark brown hair; beautiful big brown eyes that always were cheerful; gorgeous full lips with a kind smile; an elegant small nose (majority in Iran have big noses); and a stunning personality. She was about five-foot-two and 110 pounds. She dressed stylishly and elegantly, with great taste in colors. Her dresses were fashionable, but simple and chic. Her name was Bahar ... Bahar.

I watched her in the classroom and outside in the campus yard. She always was with two other girls; one was her age, Maryam, and one older, Ms. Karimnejat, who was a high school teacher in Sari. After brief investigation, I found out Bahar's older friend was a relative of my cousin's wife. This relationship helped me to learn more about Bahar and her family from Ms. Karimnejat. I explained to Ms. Karimnejat my deep interest to know Bahar, and Ms. Karimnejat talked with Bahar about me. A few weeks later, I wrote a letter to Bahar explaining my deep feeling for her, and that I wished to know her more.

Sometimes, because of the lack of time, I had to come to classes wearing my uniform. In general, people of Iran liked and respected military officers. I knew the head of the college cafeteria and asked him to treat Bahar the best possible way when she came for meals at the cafeteria. Out of respect, he obliged. Bahar did not know this arrangement, and each time when she and her two friends came for meals, the other two received regular meals, and Bahar received a much bigger plate of food or sandwich. They all wondered why Bahar got more than her friends.

We started dating in the middle of our second year at college and were together most of the time on campus. Babolsar the home of our college is a beautiful Caspian Sea city with beautiful beaches and great restaurants. On our first date, we were driving back from the Caspian Sea shore in my car, a Paykan, forest green, Persian-made car, and were deep in conversation. My focus was on Bahar, not on my driving. Our car went off the road and became stuck in the sand and I couldn't get it back onto the road. After about twenty minutes of waiting for someone to drive by, a big truck with five or six young men who were returning from work stopped, picked up the front and back of the car, and moved it to the road. It was a most embarrassing event for a first date.

It was a nice sunny day, on our second date, we were driving on the beach, I asked, "Would you like to sing a song?" Bahar replied, "No, do you want to sing?" I grabbed the opportunity and said, "Yes." I was chewing a gum, throw it away and started to sing not one, three songs. I guess I did a good job ... at least, my impression was that she liked my singing. She might pretend she liked my singing. We have told these two first and second dates' stories and laughed with each other and others for many times over the years.

Bahar talked about me with her family members, and we learned that her father, Mr. Reza Nasri, knew my father for the short time he was working in Shahi. My friend, Officer Amir Hossain Ahmadian, without my knowledge, went to Mr. Nasri's office, and talked about my character and commitment to work, life, and family. Amir's intention was to help me by explaining to Bahar's father what a good husband I would be for Bahar, and how deeply I loved her. Later, when I met with Bahar's parents, I thought they both liked me and approved of my personal and professional life.

Over the next six months, we got to know each other well. We drove together to school, enjoyed great food in the restaurants at the Caspian Sea shore after class, and drove back to Sari.

Bahar and I planned to marry in summer of 1972, six months after our first date. We went to Tehran to purchase wedding dress and other things needed for our wedding, and Bahar's mom and my older sister, Mahtob, joined us. We stayed in the home of my friends from childhood, Hassan and Ali Mobini. Those two were friends that sometimes in weekend I stayed at their apartment when I was student at the military academy. They were great hosts and did the best they could to make sure Bahar and her family were comfortable during their stay.

The invitations were sent, and everything was ready for our wedding on July 28, 1972, at Bahar's home. All family members from both sides and many friends and officers attended the wedding, including Hadi Naji, my roommate from military academy, who came from Tehran, and my friend officer Amir Hossain Ahmadian.

A band played at our wedding, with a young singer by the name of Maziar. His voice and performance were exceptional. The guests enjoyed his performance and dinner. It was a special day and night for us, and both families made great contributions. In the last 46 years, the pictures of the wedding have reminded us how our love, commitment, and journey have started and how greatly we carried our pledged and promised to each other.

We did not see the wedding singer Maziar until a few years later, when we would see him almost every day on television. He went on to become one of the most famous singers of Iran. Maziar was from Babol, and his family and friends were living in Babol. At the same time, I transferred from Sari to Babol. Maziar heard that I transferred to Babol, and the first time he came to see me, he asked if I remembered that he sang at my wedding. Each time Maziar came to Babol to visit his family, he stopped by my office for a tea and a talk about his future activities. A few times, he came to my house and brought signed pictures of himself for me to give to the children of my and

Bahar's family members. A few years ago, I heard that he died from heart attack when he was in his late fifties. We have his records, and Bahar and I, on occasion, listen to his voice and remember him and our wedding.

After the wedding, Bahar and I temporarily lived at her family's home in an extra room on the second floor. Living at Bahar's home helped both of us to focus more on our college assignments and save some money. I always appreciated and never forgot their kindness and thoughtfulness to let us stay with them until we found our own place, a small house with two bedrooms in the west of Sari.

Wedding, Bahar and Sam

6

Mystery Escape,

Officer and Terrorists, Russia

I was the third-year students at Academy, one morning around 10:00 I was called

to the reception office. I had a visitor, young man Amir Hossain Ahmadian from Shahi.

He was younger brother of my high school classmate, and one of best Gymnast in

country. A year before he won 6 gold medals in national high school championship. He

told me he was accepted to Physical Education College and the Military Academy. Each

year, Military Academy accepted a few national champions without entrance test, and

Amir was accepted without taking the entrance test. Amir asked a few questions about

Academy, its training, education, and sport activities. We talked about an hour, he told

me after consultation with his family will make his final decision about which of the

two colleges he would attend in the fall.

After my graduation from Academy, one evening in the street of Shahi, I saw

Amir the young gymnastic champion and his brother Hamid. Amir told me, after

consultation with family and evaluation of his two choices of colleges, he made decision

to go to the Military Academy and appreciated my input. I congratulated him for going

to college and wished him great success in the Academy. I did not see Amir for another

93

three years. In fall 1970, two graduated officers assigned to our prison, one of them was

Amir. Each young lieutenant had assignment to oversee about 70 officer and to serve 24

hours shift with 24 hours off. Amir was tough officer with those prisoners that

undermined the rules and daily activities. He was also trying hard to help those

prisoners that needed medical or legal support. He was generous and kind young man

with his family members and his close friends including me. Amir and I had many

shared memories; trip to see my older brother in Behshar, swimming at Caspian Sea,

eating and drinking at restaurants there, exercising at prison, and executing daily

operations. I talked about Bahar with Amir and indicated that I am not sure how her

parents were thinking about me. Amir without my knowledge, one day stopped by at

Justice Department to see Bahar's dad. Amir explained to Mr. Sofi how fine gentleman I

was, how much I loved her daughter, and how good husband I could be for her. He

also asked Mr. Sofi to not share with me his visit. After wedding, Mr. Sofi told about

Amir's visit and his deep commitment to his friend. He was a helpful and generous

friend. When he found out I need some financial help for the wedding expenses, he

loaned me about $400.00. Before leaving Iran, I stopped by at Amir's home and paid the

amount that I borrowed from Amir to his older brother.

In the fall of 1972, our prison was housing about fifty political prisoners, some

dangerous. This group used explosives to damage businesses and government

buildings, and they assassinated influential and government leaders who were against their ideologies. By today's standards they would be called terrorists. In the political

prisoner section at Sari prison were two engineering students. Because of his shared

discontent with the Shah's government, Amir communicated often and developed a

secret friendship with them.

Russia was the key player in brainwashing our young people, especially our young

college students, by giving them false hope for a better future as a communist country.

Russia was also had a great concern about influence and present of American business

and military in Iran. They distributed propaganda encouraging the use of force and

resistance against Shah and his government. In addition to providing financial support

and weapons to this group, Russia opened its borders with Iran as a safe haven for

Iranian terrorists and provided training grounds.

Prisoners were allowed visitors once a week at a defined time. One of the

political prisoners had a beautiful sister who visited frequently his brother at the days

that Amir was in the charge. She and Amir became friends, which developed into a

romantic relationship. Amir met the young woman and her other family members away

from the prison, without the knowledge of his friends, his family members, and fellow

officers. The two prisoners' families and Amir rented a house at Behshar, about twenty

miles east of Sari. For six months, Amir spent most of his free time at the house with the

terrorist's sister and a few others who came from Tehran.

The group including Amir decided to develop a plan for the escape of the two terrorists from the highly secure Sari prison. Amir agreed to join the group and then

disappear with them after the escape. (Some of the details of the escape that follow

came from Amir, who got in touch with me eight years later when I was in America and

he had returned to Iran after revolution.) They developed a detailed map of the prison,

with the positions of the all the cells and the guards.

The escape team also developed detailed information about the schedules for the

changing of the guards, other officers' assignments and schedules, and weekend

activities of the prison. A prisoner who was waiting execution was selected to set their

plan in motion. They also developed a backup plan and selected the date for the escape.

The plan included one getaway car at the prison, a change of cars in Shahi, a change of

cars again in Tehran, and then to stay in designated hiding places along their planned

route for getting out of country and into Russia.

For several months, the team, including Amir, continued improving the plan and

related details for accuracy and recovery from any unexpected situations. Finally, in late

fall of 1972, they were ready to implement their plan. In Iran, Fridays were considered

the weekend. Every Thursday after 2:00 p.m., the three higher-ranking officers left the

prison until Saturday morning. If there was any unusual situation or emergency, the

officer in charge would contact his three superiors for instructions or assistance.

Occasionally, higher-ranking officers were contacted by phone with a brief report from

an officer in charge. Around seventy guards were on duty in each shift. Amir and another young officer had a 24-hour shift, starting from 8:00 a.m. The execution of the escape plan started one Friday morning as Amir began his usual weekend shift.

Two senior guards were sitting at the front office with the officer in charge. The senior guards were assistants to officer, managing operations and overseeing changes of the guards. Amir's plan was to create an emergency situation to manipulate the guards' positions and their regular schedules. That Friday evening at 8:00 pm, he gathered the guards and informed them that one of the highly-recognized prisoners, who was sentenced to death, would be executed the next morning. Amir told the guards that the prisoner was aware of his imminent execution, and that he heard there was a plan to create chaos inside of the prison to free the prisoner and prevent the execution.

Amir told the guards to keep everything secret, and that he might rearrange their scheduled positions, shifts, and times of the shift-changes, based on the needs and future events. The guards were on edge. They believed everything that the officer in charge had told them.

Earlier that day, when all the prisoners were outdoors, Amir went inside the cell of the prisoner who was supposed to be executed the following morning and planted escape tools — a knife, an iron-cutting tool, nails, and blades —under the prisoner's bed. At 10:00 p.m., two hours after he announced the possible emergency, Amir took two senior guards to the prisoner's room and ordered the prisoner and his roommates to leave the room. He instructed the two senior guards to inspect the prisoner's bed, which resulted in the discovery of the escape tools that Amir had planted earlier.

Immediately, Amir relocated the prisoner to a special individual cell. Now the guards

had no doubt about what Amir had told them about execution and possible escape.

At 11:00 p.m., the two terrorists who were supposed to escape with Amir started

fighting and making noise in their cell. Amir brought the two to his office, screamed at

them, and told them they would be severely punished the next morning. He moved

them to a temporary cell next to office, slapped their faces, and told the guards to not

give them blankets for sleeping. The temporary cell was for the new prisoners to be

prepared for moving to the main cells.

Regulation for changing guards called for the replacement guard to report to the

assignment point, take charge, inform the officer or senior guards (assistant) in the

office, then the guard from the previous shift would leave his post. At 12:00 midnight,

the time of the change in shift, Amir told the four guards in the four towers around the

prison to leave their posts and report immediately to his office. Amir told them their

replacements were helping elsewhere inside the prison but would cover their posts

within a few minutes.

He then ordered the guards patrolling outside the prison building to go

immediately to the inside the woodwork factory, close the door, and make sure none of the dangerous tools got into the hands of the prisoners. He told them they did not have to wait for their replacements, that he would send them a few minutes later. The towers and around the outside of building were left without guards. Amir sent the guards who came from towers to the cells at the far side of the prison away from other guards.

When the replacement guards arrived, Amir told them he had told the guards already on duty on towers and patrolling outside to remain on their shifts for a few more hours--that he needed the next shift to cover positions inside the dining area, which had an easy way out from the building to the prison's open area.

Meanwhile, news was spreading inside the prison that a convicted prisoner would be executed the next morning. Amir sent many guards inside the prison hallway to patrol, in order to show the prisoners in their locked cells that the guards were in full control. Amir sent the two senior guards that were in his office, who usually took over the charge when Amir or officer in charge went for nap, to eat, or shower, to the kitchen's cooking area, where the kitchen knives and other sharp tools were locked up.

By now, Amir was the only one left in the front office. All the guards believed they were in emergency situations, and that the shift changes were taking place as usual, but with a few minutes' delay. He divided, so cleverly, the guards into different sections of the prison, so that the replacement and previous shift guards could not see each other. The assumption among the guards was that every position was covered and protected by the usual guards, as scheduled.

Amir locked all three doors in the hallway leading to the main cells and dining area and took the keys. He had driven a rented car to work that day, which was parked inside the property, in front of the office. At 1:00 a.m., Amir opened the door of the temporary cell next to his office, and he and the two terrorists took a few hand guns and ammunition, got into the rental car, and left through the prison's entrance door, leaving the large metal doors half close. Then they threw away the keys to the hallways and to the cells and drove to Amir's home in Shahi, where a second rental car was parked.

Amir told his family that he had a major assignment and would be gone for a few days. He and the two terrorists then transferred their belongings and weapons to the second car. By early morning, they reached Tehran, left the car in a vacant area, and drove yet another car, which no one would be able to trace. They arrived at a designated secret hiding place in Tehran, and disappeared for years to come, without a trace.

At the prison early the next morning, the guards in the front hallway noticed the front gate of the prison was open, and that a few cows from a neighboring farm were in the prison yard. The guards were afraid to make too much noise about it, which would alert the prisoners that something unusual had happened and create a dangerous situation for the guards. The hallway doors were locked, so they informed the guards in the dining area about the opened front door and the cows and asked them to tell the situation to the senior guards who were in the kitchen. At first, the dining guards thought they were joking, and throwing pieces of cheeses to them. Finally, the guards in the hallway convinced the guards in the dining area of the seriousness of the situation, they informed the two senior guards who were in the kitchen area about the open door and the cows in the prison yard.

The kitchen door to the outside yard had a glass window and no metal bars. The two officer helpers broke the glass, slid through the broken window to outside, and rushed to the front office. They found no one in the office; the front door, office door and the door of the ammunitions room were wide open.

Afraid and confused, they expected to find something bad had happened to Officer Amir Hossain Ahmadian. They called his name and searched for him, but did not find him. The guards thought he was killed or had been kidnapped as a hostage.

Picture with AMIR, Caspian Sea

Around 5:30 a.m., I received an emergency call from senior guards in the prison.

Within ten minutes I arrived at the prison and received an ambiguous report of Amir's

disappearance. The two other head officers arrived, and we were informed about the

execution plan of a prisoner, how guards were locked in different areas of the prison,

and that all keys were missing. We immediately informed the general, the head of state,

and summoned a locksmith to break open the doors in order to bring out the guards

from the inside hallways of the prison. We searched every room, the factory, the towers,

and all around the prison for Officer Ahmadian, but did not find him. We kept the

prisoners in their cells, they were counted, and we discovered that two political

prisoner terrorists were missing. We also discovered some of the ammunition and guns

were missing too. When we heard of the fake story of an execution and the unusual changing of the guards, it became certain that Amir was part of the plan for the terrorists' escape.

In the modern history of Iran, this was only the second time an officer was a traitor to Shah and the military. The first time was after WWII when an officer escaped to Russia, which was an embarrassment to the Iranian government, military, and Shah. This was worse — it involved an officer and two terrorist prisoners. The matter was so treacherous that Shah was informed immediately, and before noon, three generals came from Tehran to evaluate the situation and report detailed facts to Shah.

I was selected to give the initial salute and report of the situation to the generals. This was the worst possible situation for formal reporting, and I was nervous about possible unexpected reactions of the three generals. The escape was a great mystery, with much confusion about how it could have happened. Naturally, my friendship with Amir identified me as a person who might know about the plans and was hiding some information. I was asked to remain for three days at the prison for investigation. Amir's brothers, father, and mother were all apprehended for questioning. I just married a few months ago, it was such a terrifying event for Bahar and her and my families. As part of leadership of the prison, I had to carry the shell-shock of this unexpected situation inside and underlying bitterness emotion created inside anxiety and anger. With precise investigation it was clear that I had not had any role or any knowledge about the whole event, but I felt that the lingering suspicious existed as long as I was working in the prison.

After a few days, I received an assignment, along with a few guards, to take Amir's entire family to Tehran for further investigation. I was not sure why they assigned me the task of the transfer to Tehran, where I was a person of interest in the escape for authorities. I was friends with Amir's brother and knew all the family members. I was certain the family did not have any knowledge about Amir's escape plan, but I could not be any help. The Amir family were scared for Amir's safety and life, and for their own future. I could see from their face that they wanted to ask many questions about the event, but instructions were no conversation and discuss of the escape. Without incident, I transported the family to Tehran to the central office. The escape and Amir's disappearance became a mystery that could not be solved by local and federal investigations.

My assignment at the prison was changed with less daily involvement in leadership activities. I suppose I remained a suspect. Mentally and emotionally I had hard time coming to the prison each day to carry my new assignments. I knew that I was not involved and did not know anything about Amir's plan, but I could see the doubt in some of the prisoners' and guards' eyes and comments.

The decrease in responsibilities gave me more time to focus on my studies and personal life. Meanwhile, we received classified information that Amir was leading a group that carried out dangerous assignments against the Iranian government and influential people.

A few months later, Bahar and I travelled to Astera, a city in northwest of Iran, to visit my older brother, Saleh, who had recently transferred from Behshar as the head of the bank. When Saleh was at Behshar, a year before Amir's escape, Amir and I had stayed in his home for a few days. Amir knew Saleh and assumed he was still working at Behshar. Upon our arrival in Astera, Saleh told us that a few weeks earlier, he had a visitor in his new office in Astera, the head of local Savak (secret service). Saleh had received his daily mail while the visitor was there, and in the mail, was an envelope from bank of Behshar. He opened it and found a smaller envelope inside. He opened the smaller envelope, and at the top of the enclosed letter, he saw, "Dear Sam." He glanced to the end of the letter and read, "Goodbye forever. Signed, Amir Hossain Ahmadian." The letter was received about 20 days after Amir's disappearance.

Saleh was so afraid; his face became pale. His house was on the second floor of the bank, and he explained to his visitor that he was not feeling well and had to go upstairs for a few minutes to take medicine. Amir was the most wanted man in the country, and the cause of the biggest manhunt in modern Iran. Saleh knew that I was suspect, and this letter could make the situation even worse for me.

When Saleh was upstairs, he quickly read the two-page letter from Amir, then burned it immediately. Saleh told me that Amir, in great length, apologized for his actions, which had put all of us in danger. Amir explained that after escape from prison, he stayed in a secure place in Tehran for ten days. He indicated that he had written the letter and mailed it on the last day of his stay in Tehran, and before his escape to Russia, with the help of an underground network. I didn't hear from Amir until he called me when I was living in the United States years later. The following Amir's Phone call and conversation clear mystery and details of the above escape.

In spring of 1980, I received a long-distance call. When I heard the voice on the other end of the line, I could not believe it. It was Amir Hossain Ahmadian, the officer who escaped with two prisoners many years ago from our prison in Sari, Iran. The only time I had heard from him between the time he'd escaped and now was through the letter he'd sent to my brother that my brother burned instead of giving it to me. The only other news I had about him was classified information by the Iranian Government — that he was the head of an assassination team of the Fadaian Khalgh, the underground group directed and funded by Russia against Shah and his government.

Amir and I talked for about an hour. He began the conversation by saying how deeply sorry he was to put me and other friends in difficult situations, and then explained the events that had taken place before and after the escape. Much of the information he shared had been a mystery, even to the investigating authorities. After hearing his side of the event, I could be the only one knew the whole story from both sides.

He told me that he'd hid for about ten days in Tehran, until his transfer to Russia became ready. His main training was in Russia and East Germany. Amir said he came back frequently to Iran with assignments to cause damage to the government or to assassinate influential leadership. Each time, after he completed his assignment, he'd go back into hiding in Lebanon or Palestine. He asked, "Sam, did you receive the letter I sent to you before leaving Iran?" He continued, "I sent to your brother in Behshar, not direct to you." I replied, "No I did not read the letter, but my brother shared the content with me." He said, "I wanted to make sure to say sorry and good bye." I laughed, and said, "Do not worry, we both are perusing a new life." We also talked about our families in Iran.

After the revolution, Amir returned to Iran as a hero. He wrote a book and was asked to speak in universities and at national events. He said Khomani promised to let the people of Iran run the country, and not religion, but his supporters stole the revolution, took over all phases of governing the country, and pressured and created tension for the Fadaian Khalgh, who were the primary fighters in the revolution. Amir said Fadaian Khalgh members were ready to go underground and to start their new adventure with the Khomani's government. We said goodbye, wished someday we be able to see, have a glass of vodka, and talk about life.

I have not heard anything from Amir, until in 1990 when I traveled with my family to Sweden to see my three brothers and their families. In Upsala, Sweden, my younger brother told me that he heard Amir is in Sweden and asked me, do I want he finds out where Amir is and let Amir knows I am in Uppsala. I told him no, it could be dangerous for family, and might agents from other countries surveillance Amir.

7

New Assignment,

Liberation from Prison

In 1974, eighteen months after Amir's escape, I was still working in the Sari prison and impatiently waiting for a break to be transferred to a new city with a new assignment. It was our last year of college and Bahar was pregnant with our first child. The last few months had been really tough for her to travel every day from Sari to Babolsar, attend classes, and to do all the assignments.

In the last month of her pregnancy, we were hoping the baby would be born after all the final exams. We successfully passed all subjects, and only one exam was left to graduate. The night before the last exam, Bahar started to have labor pains. At 10:00 p.m., I drove her to the doctor's home in Sari. The doctor told me it was delivery time, and to take Bahar to Shahi's Hospital. The doctor followed us to the hospital, and many family members, including Bahar's mom, and my mom, came to the hospital.

We all gathered in the waiting room and anxiously waited for news. The doctor informed us that he needed to perform a Caesarean section to save the baby and Bahar. It was a nervous time for all of us. At 2:00 a.m., May 24, 1974, our beautiful daughter, Sheila, was born.

I took the Micro Economics exam at 2:00 p.m. on May 24, 1974 — twelve hours after Sheila was born. Bahar and I made the decision that I would take the exam and tell the professor what had happened. The professor was kind and understanding, agreed that Bahar could take the test a week later. We both passed the exam and received our B.A. degree in Economy.

Around this time, Colonel Malik Mohammedi, a fine gentleman, had transferred from Tehran to Sari. He was in line to become chairman of forces in one of the larger cities in the state. To keep the forces in the good physical shape, he suggested a daily morning exercise. Fortunately, my name was forwarded to him when he asked for a recommendation for an athletic officer to lead the new daily physical activities.

The colonel asked me to develop a plan of daily exercises for all the officers in Sari, and to be in charge of implementing the plan. The new assignment was a great fit with my background and gave me some relief from my unchallenging assignment in the prison, as well as new recognition in the leadership.

Every morning, for about 45 minutes, I led the exercises of all members of the forces in a soccer field in Sari. The colonel was impressed with my commitment, plans, effort, and execution. Meanwhile, we developed a friendship and discussed future. He knew I was not happy with my current assignments and was ready for a new challenging opportunity. He indicated that he would like to transfer me with him when he received his new assignment in the near future. In the last week of morning exercise, when we tried to move soccer goal pole, it dropped on my foot and broke my toe. After a few days, I was able to walk with a cast and continued my daily assignments.

After a few months, Colonel Mohammedi accepted a new assignment as the chairman of forces in Babol and transferred me from the Sari prison to Babol. I was so happy that after seven years I was done dealing with prison and prisoners. It was a joyful opportunity for Bahar and me to leave the last two years of the gloominess caused by the Amir's escape and restart a new assignment in a new city with positive attitude to contribute with excellence services. As 21 years old 2nd lieutenant officer I got assignment to lead over 70 guards and to execute rules of law and implement restrict procedures in the daily life of over 1,000 lawless, dangerous, uncontrollable prisoners that already broken law in the society. It is impossible for public to imagine the needed toughness and strength for this job. As 21 years old, you must be as tough as nails to endure for many years the mental and physical suffering of controlling over 1,000 prisoners. Prisoners try to survive violent in a ferocious world of prison and guards try to prevent violent not only to prisoners, but also to themselves. When there were about over 50 murders in the prison, there is not limitation for violent and there is not any effective rules to deal with it.

I had friends in Babol, and some of my mother's relatives were living there. Babol is a business-oriented city with many rich and influential people. I was put in charge of security, crime, and city protection, a job similar to chief of police in America, but with more authority, power, and responsibilities. I had more than 100 officers under my command and a driver, who was dedicated to work with me full-time, and help with my family's transportation needs.

Already having adequate knowledge of the city and knowing influential people and most of the officers — and some of the criminals — made my job effective from the first day of the assignment. Criminals and drug dealers shifted their focus on the areas outside of my jurisdictions, and robbers and street fighters avoided me. I had a few informants from past prisoners who knew most criminals and their styles. They were extremely helpful to prevent crimes and capture criminals. If a crime happened in the city, in addition to investigations by my officers, a few informants were assigned to gather information.

I continued to serve under Colonel Mohammedi for the next five years and appreciated his support and help. He was a good leader, gentleman, helpful and supportive of his officers, and he was a great friend.

Although I was busy with work and my family life, I managed to find some time for sports. I established a soccer club (PAS), for young players, an extension of the famous PAS Soccer Club in Tehran that had won a few national and Asian championships. The club required extra time and commitment, but it was fun and was a great service to the community.

Picture of Soccer Team

I also continued to coach the boxing team, participated a few practices a week. I coached the state boxing team in national championship for the next four years.

Community service and helping others with different needs made me pleased. During my four years as a student at Babolsar, I may have been the most well-known officer in the region. I born and grew in Shahi, my father was from city of the city of Amol, my mother was from the city of Babol, and Bahar was from Sari. These four cities were about fifty miles range and many relatives were living on those cities. Whenever Bahar and I went shopping or out to restaurants, we received the best services and compliments from the business owners. The regional recognition and having social influence made it possible for me to help friends and family with their many different demands and needs.

My father enjoyed my status in society and was very proud of me. After he retired from government, he took a job as director of hospital in Amol. A few times a week, he traveled between from Shahi to Babol, then from Babol to Amol, which was about 30 miles each trip. The drivers competed to have him in their car. Sometimes, instead of taking him from Babol Station to Amol Station directly, they brought him by my office. On the way, sometimes they explained to my father what kind of business or legal problems they had and asked him for advice and help.

When my father came into our central office, the officer in the front saluted him. No matter what I was doing, my staff knew I was always available when my father came in. It would be disrespectful to my father if I sat behind my desk in his presence, so I always rushed to greet him and sat on a chair next to him. I would see in my father's eyes how proud he was when he saw me in uniform and what I could do in the region for others. He would tell me about his drivers' problems and recommended that I help. After I promised to help, he'd return to the driver and continue to Amol. I had to do what I promised, because he would see the driver the next day and would be informed of the results.

One day, the officer in charge came into my office and told me Mr. Abdullah Movahed was there with his wife to see me. Mr. Movahed was the most well-known wrestling champion in the world. He had won six Olympic and World championships and had been retired from wrestling for a few years. He was a candidate to coach American national team. I greeted them and invited them for tea.

Mr. Movahed explained that his wife would like to get her driver's license and needed my help to facilitate the process. Those days, getting a license could take a few months. The waiting list to take the written exam was about a month. After passing the written exam, you would be scheduled for the driving exam, which could take another

month or more.

I called the bureau and asked my good friend, Captain Cheetgar, for help. Then I

sent an officer with Mr. Movahed to the bureau office. It took only one hour for Mrs.

Movahed to receive her driver's license. Before leaving the city, he stopped by in the

office and appreciated the help.

The next time Mr. Movahed came to see me, he told me there was a great new

addition of lots for sale in Babolsar along the Caspian Sea. He said the land was

divided, and many influential people already had purchased pieces of the land. He

encouraged me to purchase a lot to build a vacation home. He recommended me to the

seller, and I bought a lot near Mr. Movahed's lot.

One of my childhood friends, Parviz Nearohe — one of the nicest people in the

world — came to see me one day at my office. He owned a store near my parent's

home, and he and his five children often helped my parents with chores and services.

Parviz told me he was bankrupt, had sold his store to pay his debts, and he was out of a

job. With a family of five, he desperately needed a job. Fortunately, a few days earlier, a

top executive of the electric company, who was my friend, came to my office and asked

for a favor. He was building a house in Sari and needed materials from a factory in

Babol. The factory manager told him it would take three months to deliver the needed materials. This top executive asked me to use my influence to help him receive the needed building materials as soon as possible. I promised I would help him within a few days.

After hearing Parviz's story, I called the factory in Babol. The owner, who knew me, said he was delighted to help and would send the needed materials to Sari by the next week. I called the electric company executive in Sari and told him he would receive the needed building materials by the next week, and that I would send my childhood friend, who needed a job desperately, to him to be hired as soon as possible. He said he needed a daily driver to take him for visits around the state. He hired Parviz the same day, with a good annual salary.

Parviz appreciated it and said driving for the executive was his dream job. Many times when Parviz drove executives to Babol, he stopped in my office to see me and tell me how great his life had become. The same executive friend hired Bahar and my sister, Nazenin. Both worked at the electric company for a short time, until they became teachers in Sari and Babol.

In addition to those three, two other childhood friends from my street were hired by this wonderful executive. Those days, to know influential people in Iran and make recommendations had great weight in hiring.

It was 1975, the last few months, I had not heard anything from Bahman. Until, I heard that there was conflict between government security forces and Bahman and Cathy. Bahman and Cathy were killed in the conflict by security forces when they took refuge in a cave. The circumstance of their death was unclear and caused many different stories. I heard their daughter was safe and was living with her grandparents in Tehran. Cathy and Bahman were two very special people, with great hearts and beautiful minds. They left a luxurious lifestyle to live a simple life as farmers, living with farmers, and sharing everything with them as a family. I have always admired them and imagine them being together in heaven with big smiles.

When Bahar started as a teacher in the girls' high school, we bought a lot in a nice part of Babol to build a beautiful house and rented a house near the school. At the time, Bahar was pregnant with our second child. My friend, Dr. Koshanfar, who was a surgeon and Bahar's physician, had his practice in Sari. On December 6, 1976, Bahar and I went to hospital in Sari. All family from both sides gathered in the waiting room. Dr. Koshanfar informed us Bahar needed a Caesarean section to deliver the baby. Our beautiful daughter, Shadi, which means "happiness," was born at 3:00 p.m.

With a beautiful wife and two healthy daughters, I was the luckiest man alive.

In addition to family and work, Bahar and I started to become financially stable. We built a beautiful house in Babol that was marble on the outside, and then sold it for a profit. We invested the profit to buy land and build another house in Sari, which we also sold for a profit. With the extra savings, we bought land between Shahi and Sari, which had great potential. We had bought the lot on the Caspian Sea for a future vacation home, and bought a lot in Babol to build our dream home. To expand our wealth, we participated in the State of Mazandaran plans to build houses for teachers in designated sections in each city. Bahar paid a down payment for a house in the teachers' subdivision in Shahi.

Finally, we bought a 5-acre lot in a rural area near the Caspian Sea, close to city of Farah Abad. On one side of the land was a river that flowed to the Caspian Sea, and on the other side was the sea shore. We planted over 500 fruit trees, which we imagined would be a great investment for the future. We started building our dream home in Babol, with four bedrooms and three bathrooms with a three-car garage below about six months before the revolution.

8

Start of Revolution

In the early part of the twentieth century, Ahmad Shah Qajar, from the Qajar

Dynasty, lost many of Iran's integral areas to Russia, including parts of Georgia,

Azerbaijan, and Armenia, and some parts of Afghanistan and Uzbekistan to the British.

The country was in chaos and disorder and needed a new leader to secure borders,

unify the country, and bring order to the society.

Shah's father, Reza Shah, was the greatest patriot our ancient country ever had. In

1925, General Reza Pahlavi started a critically needed revolution to establish the Pahlavi

Dynasty. He believed in the separation of religion from government, and that religious

practices be conducted only in the mosque, not in public or in schools. He tried to create

a civil and educated society similar to European countries, creating universities and

sending selected students in different disciplines around the world to bring new ideas

and perspectives to Iran.

To strengthen productivity, Reza Shah brought women into the work force, forced

them to wear European style cloths, and built many new factories in different parts of

the country. He relocated workers to supply needed manpower, created hospitals in

each city, developed a national railway system, and created many government branches

to centralize and harmonize national agendas.

To advance the architectural design of cities, Reza Shah ordered implementation of a new plan for most of the cities to build unified, magnificent governmental offices, a beautiful town square and buildings with meaningful architecture, main streets, and railway stations. Iran had many different regions, each with their own languages, cultures, and rules. He brought all those separated regions under unified federal rules and made Farsi the national language.

In World War II, he announced Iran as a neutral country, and did not compromise with the Russia and West to use Iran's territories and its resources to fight Germany. In 1941, the Russia and West leaders met in Tehran, sent him into exile in Johannesburg, South Africa. He died in exile in 1944 and Iran lost its greatest visionary and leader. If Iran could have another 15 years of his leadership, Iran could be one of the most advanced industrial and prosperous country in the world.

Following his exile, his 22-year-old son, Mohammad Reza Pahlavi, became the Shah of Iran. He was a western-educated young man with little experience and, unlike his father, was not tough. He was kind, compassionate, thoughtful, and had a deep commitment to religion and a close friendship with the West, especially with America.

Iran had long land and sea borders with Russia, and the friendship with America, and having over 50,000 American experts in all different divisions such as oil, military, etc. in Iran America's present in Iran was a major concern for the Russians. In those days, Russia was involved in many underground strategies and activities in order to damage the Shah and Iranian government. Simply, the world would have been a much nicer place if communist ideology did not exist.

The Shah of Iran was rushing to advance all phases of education, society, and culture. He encouraged the younger generations to seek education around the world. He provided stipends to help the expenses. He also encouraged students to come back to visit Iran during their studies abroad by providing free return trips and guaranteed almost all would have jobs after graduating and returning to Iran.

He added many new universities in Iran, most of them free of tuition and other expenses for all accepted students. He changed the law to give equal opportunities to women in education, social rights, and jobs even in arm forces. Shah's government designed and created a great program for social and educational advancement of the rural and villages. The program sent the young servicemen to carry the two-year mandatory military services in villages and rural communities to help in education and health of rural people. He redesigned the land ownership, transferring the lands from rich owners to the farmers who worked on those lands.

To reduce drug distributions, he changed the laws. If a dealer was found with more than two pounds of drugs, that dealer would be tried at the military court, not the civil court, which could mean life in prison or execution. Each of these rapid changes created oppositions for the government and Shah.

When I was in charge of the prison, I had over 50 prisoners from the government and the Shah-opposing groups causing all the conflict: the majority were from Fadaian Khalgh, Sacrifice for People Cause, and the Mojahedin Khalgh, Soldiers of Holy War. These groups were assembled mostly by young people and college students.

In the last few years in Iran, both groups made frequent problems for government and forces, but, as earlier stated, we had orders from the federal government to compromise as much as possible and to use minimum force against them. The reason for this strategy, again, was the Shah and government of Iran believed the foolishness was temporary, and that with more advancement in the economy and social life, the general public would not support the radical groups and young people would not join them.

The Shah and government assessment of the future was wrong. Outside governments and religious leaders extended their destruction and operations with more propaganda and more deadly attacks.

One day, I was called to a car accident outside of the city. The driver was hurt, and we tried to help and send him to the hospital. He rejected our help; instead, he was more concerned about his car and insisted on leaving the accident sight. He could

barely talk. I asked him a few questions, and against his wishes, I sent him to the

hospital. He was 18 years old and in his first year in college.

When we inspected his car, we found a handgun and explosives. He was coming

to Babol with plans to damage a building or assassinate a person in charge. We placed

him under arrest and later moved him to the prison.

Russia was destroying our young, intelligent minds, sacrificing their future and

their lives for the wrong reasons. Most of the young people who joined Fadaian Khalgh

were the best young minds and students in our top universities. The focus of Russian

propaganda was on the young men from low income-families and the religious leaders'

focus was on the uneducated young men from religious families. During my youth, Iran

did not have many universities and only the top five to ten percent could attend

universities, with tuition, food, and dorms all free, paid by government.

One of the students who graduated in my high school class was a very quiet and

excellent student named Jafar. He was the oldest son from a poor family. His father sold

nuts on the street corner to support his family. Jafar was the hope of his family for a

better future. He had been accepted into the University of Tehran, the best university in

the Middle East. He joined the Fadaian Khalgh and was killed during an attack on government agencies. At the time of his death, Jafar was a third-year student in the university. His family was devastated. Their hope for a better future was gone.

As I continued my work in Babol, we received frequent instructions about increased of underground activities in our areas. The groups started to organize frequent public gatherings and, in some cases, arranged demonstrations in the streets.

Around this time, movies and circuits were a great treat for people. A circuit came to Babol for a few night programs. The first night of the show, a group of more than fifty of these extremists gathered outside and threatened to burn the circuit. With thirty officers, we broke the gathering and forced them to go home.

The second night, the opposition group had grown to over two hundred, some with torches in hand ready to burn the circuit while families with children already were inside enjoying the show. If we had been allowed to use force, we could easily have brought this dangerous situation under control.

I talked with some of the leaders and they regarded me as somebody who is helpful, tough, and fair. I reminded them that if they attack the circuit full of the families with children, I would have to retaliate with extreme force, and, if needed, would kill some of them. I also promised to end the program early and to cancel the scheduled performance of the next night.

Fortunately, without any bloodshed and destruction, we ended this dangerous situation, but the pressure to compromise with the opposition was becoming too much for me. I could not sleep well kept wishing for permission to capture leaders, and, by force, prevent the gathering and the destructions of properties of the people and government. With lack of force's retaliation, the opposition groups got bullied and started daily demonstration in the main business hubs of Babol. In early days of demonstrations, when I stopped by on the scene with a few officers, the demonstration disbanded immediately, but after a few times when they found out we would not use forces, the gathering got bigger, and in some cases, they started destructions of properties. My biggest fear was the bullied oppositions develop plan to harm the officers.

9

Unfair Assassination,

Rough Chase of Terrorists

In 1978, activities from underground opposition groups were on the rise. Fortunately, weapons were not readily available, as we see in America today. The opposition groups received weapons and ammunitions from Iranian borders, or they robbed the weapons stores in the cities.

In the fall, a robbery occurred at our weapons store at Babol. We knew something bad was about to happen soon and I always reminded our forces to be ready all the time. A young officer Hossain and his wife expected their second child to be born in less than two weeks. He asked for a day of vacation to take his wife to Chalose, a city about 50 miles from Babol. He explained that they have a 3 years old son, and his wife's parents that live in Chalose can help her pregnant wife and take care of their 3-year-old son.

Daily, with a guard and driver, I inspect the city to check the more sensitive areas, such as government buildings, schools, businesses, and to check on the guards and security officers who walked in the assigned district. In addition, once or twice a week I asked my driver, along with a guard who carried a machine gun, to pick me up at midnight in front of my home. For two to three hours, in the middle of the night, I checked the city and guards on the duties.

The nights that I inspected the city and guards on duties, I was ready at 12:00

midnight and left the home when I heard the car's engine. One night when they had

come to pick me up, I had not woken up on time. The driver made the decision to drive

around and come back fifteen minutes later. When they left my street, they were

attacked, and the passenger side of the car was shot at a few times. The terrorists knew

my schedule and thought I was sitting in the passenger side. Miraculously, no one was

hurt. I called for a major search until morning, with no success. The incident made my

wife and our families very apprehensive and worried about my safety.

A week later, I was in my office, the door to hallway was open. I saw a young man

about 6 feet tall walked a few times front of my office. I came out of my office, went to

the reception room and pretended I am not concern about the young man presence in

the hallway. From glass wall I could see him much better than from my office. He

seemed investigating the positions of the rooms, guards in charges, and activities in the

building. I asked the officer in charge of the station about the young man, he said he

was busy with a case and did not notice him. I walked to the young man and asked him

why you are here. He responded that he is waiting for his friend who had a legal

complain and supposed to meet him here. When I asked what your friend's name is and

what is the nature of complain, he became nervous and his eyes started blinking

rapidly. With unrest was growing in city, I thought it might be an assessment of the

building for future attack. I did not have any evidence to arrest him, asked the officer in charge to get his personal information and make sure he leave the building and do not

back again.

At night, we had more than twenty pairs of officers on patrol around the city. The

night shift was from 12:00 midnight to 8:00 a.m. — four hours of walking patrol, and

another four hours as back-up force in the station. Hossain, the young man that moved

his pregnant wife to Chalose was a fine officer about twenty-six years old and had been

on the force the past five years. Afternoon around 2:00, the young officer came to my

office and explained that he received a call from his wife's family that his wife is going

to go to the delivery the next day. He asked for my permission to skip the 4 hours back-

up duty, leave at 4:00 a.m. after he finished his regular walking-patrol from 12:00 to

4:00. I gave him the permission to leave and informed the officer in charge of the night

shift.

He was paired with an older officer and was excited to finish his regular patrol at

4:00 a.m. and leave for Chalose to be with his wife during delivery of their second child.

These two officers' assignment was to patrol the main market of the city from 12:00 to

4:00 a.m. The main market was in the southern corner of the city, it had a few narrow

streets with shops in both side of the streets. During day it was packed with shoppers,

and most families purchased their daily groceries from this market. Around 6:00 p.m.

the shops were closed, and the market was vacant until next morning. The area was dark in the night, only a few street lights lit the market's streets.

The city's main streets, markets, and offices all where in a less than square mile area. Usually, all the night patrol officers were at station 15 minutes before 12:00 midnight to register. They receive the instructions and weapons then the two paired officers walked to their assignment area. Hossain and the older officer walked to the market, and Hossain was explaining to the older officer that he is nervous about his pregnant wife and anxious to finish the 4 hours walking-patrol and leave immediately for Chalose. Unfortunately, three terrorists planned a deadly attack this night, and selected the market as a perfect place for their attack. As usual, two officers walked around the market, checked some of the shops to make sure they are locked, and slowly walked from one street to another one. Terrorist with guns had hidden in the corner of a dark alley and parked their getaway car in the street about 50 yards away. At 1:30 a.m., when the two officers got close to their hiding place, the terrorists shot a few times toward the officers and the young officer was badly injured. The older patrolman shot back, hitting one of the terrorists in the stomach. The other two terrorists dragged the injured one away, jumped into their car, and drove off. The unhurt officer called headquarters and reported the emergency situation. Immediately, an ambulance and several officers were sent to the scene. The injured officer was placed in the ambulance for transport to the hospital, he was shot a few times and was bleeding badly. I was

informed of the shooting by phone, and within minutes a car with my driver and two

officers armed with machine guns arrived at my home. I told the driver to take me first

to the hospital to find out about the injured officer.

The hospital front door was separated from the street by a ten-foot bridge. The

injured terrorist was losing a lot of blood, and the other two terrorists worried he might

die soon. Two unhurt terrorists, during their escape, planned to drop the injured one in

front of the hospital, then drive away. The timing for them could not be worse. They

stopped their white sedan on the bridge, and the two terrorists carried the injured one

to the door of the hospital. At the same time, my car with armed officers, reached the

bridge in front of hospital. We were rushing to go into the hospital, but the white sedan

blocked the bridge and the front door of the hospital. My driver screamed at them to

move their car —having no knowledge, of course, that they were the terrorists. When

terrorists realized who we were, they dropped the injured young man, starting shooting

at our car, and ran fast onto different streets to make it harder for us to catch them.

Once we realized that these were the terrorists who earlier shot the officers on the street,

we drove and chased one, and after a half-mile, reached him.

The houses in Iran have tall walls around them for security and privacy, which

makes it difficult to climb. When he turned and shot toward our car, my driver — an

131

old, experienced officer — hit him with the front of the car, injuring and knocking him to the ground. A second car behind us captured him and took him to the hospital. Meanwhile, four more cars with officers arrived in front of the hospital.

Meanwhile, I was informed that our young officer died when ambulance brought him to the hospital. Losing a fine young officer who was about to become a father made me very sad and mad. We unfairly lost a fine young man and a great officer with a bright future. Terrorists took away a good father from a new born baby, a great husband from his young wife, and a great serviceman from society. I could not imagine how we could relay this unfair loss to his wife and his parents. I was furious and decided that no matter what, I had to capture the third terrorist. I ordered three cars with officers to block the three exit routes from the city: north to Babolsar; west to Amol; and south to Shahi. I took ten officers with me to chase the third terrorist on foot. The end of the street that the third terrorist ran away reached a bank of river with tall grass and strong currents. It was a cloudy and dark night, which made visibility and the search much more difficult.

The search was conducted about 600 yards from the bridge, which was at the main street on the other side of the hospital and was main route to the City of Amol. We had seen the third terrorist run toward this street, but we were not sure if he had reached to the river bank or hid in one of the houses. I sent three officers to the end of the street to inspect the river bank and block the exit from the street, and I assigned

three officers to the entrance of the street. Frequently, I received reports of the search by

the three chase cars blocking the exit routes from the city of Babol.

I formed two teams, each with four officers, to inspect the 20 houses on both

sides of the street. We knocked on doors and woke up the households, went inside, and

inspected every room and the yards. In less than an hour, we completed our

inspections, and reached the bank of the river with no success. We all were

disappointed and stood at the riverbank, the officers waited for my next instruction.

Just I began to talk, we heard a loud scream coming from a house located in the

middle of this street. We ran toward the house, the door opened, and an old man

furiously told us that the terrorist was hiding in the restroom in the yard and had run

toward the house. (In Iran, some houses have a restroom inside and a restroom in the

corner of the yard, separated from the house.) All of us, including the officers on the

bank of the river, rushed to the inside of the old man's house, but the terrorist ran inside

the house, and had jumped from the kitchen window to the neighbor's wall and yard.

He jumped from a wall behind the neighbor's house, ran to the bank of the river,

through the long grass, and disappeared again into the dark night.

After another search, I came back and asked the old man where the terrorist was,

and also asked why his mouth was bloody. He explained that after the initial search, officers left his house and he went to the outside restroom. The restroom had an open, vaulted ceiling, with only the roof at the top. When he was using the restroom, he saw the terrorist on the wood rafters of the ceiling. The fugitive jumped down, hit the old man's chest with his handgun, then punched his face to keep him quiet before running toward the house.

I was very disappointed we could not capture the third killer. I drove around again to check the main streets and the three exit routes of the city. I finished the first exit route to Shahi, and with three officers and a driver, went to the Amol exit route. The exit route to Amol had a bridge over the river with rough water flowing beneath it. As we got near the bridge, we saw someone walking over the bridge; he was wet and seemed anxious. We guessed that he might be the third terrorist. My driver stopped the car about ten yards from the person walking. We drew our revolvers, ran toward him, and I ordered him not to move. He ran toward the edge of the bridge and jumped into the dark, rough water, about twenty feet below. Again, we lost track of him. We hoped he had drowned. After a one-hour search of both sides of the riverbanks, we decided to stop and to resume the chase during daylight.

I returned to the hospital and made sure both injured terrorists had adequate care, guards, and protection. I could communicate with one of the terrorists, who was from a local city, and whose father had come to the hospital. His father talked with him and convinced him to cooperate with us. He gave the name of the third terrorist and

told us he had an aunt who lived in a village about three miles from Babol toward

Amol, the village that was in the direction he disappeared during our chase. It was

around 1:00 in the afternoon that I collected all the needed information about the village

and the location of the aunt's house in the village.

After the terrorist jumped from the bridge, he'd stayed with the flow of the

water, and after a few hundred yards came out of the water, went into the woods, and

walked to the village. At 2:00 p.m., I brought twenty officers and soldiers to the village

and we surrounded the house of the fugitive's aunt. The house was in the middle of

village and a wall of about 6 feet surrounded the half acre yard of the house. I gave

instructions for everyone to stay in his designated position, and no one was to shoot or

anything else until they heard my order for action.

With my revolver in my hand and two officers with their guns in the ready

position behind me, I knocked on the door of the house a few times. The door opened,

and there stood a young man with a bare upper body and a rifle. Without hesitation,

one of the officers behind me, who became scared at the sight of the young man with

the rifle, shot the young man in the stomach. All of us thought he was the third terrorist

that we had been chasing for more than 12 hours. The young man fell to the ground and

was losing blood fast from his wound.

After the gunshot, a few people ran from inside the home toward the door, and an old man screamed that this was his son, who was a navy soldier. All the officers who had surrounded the house left their positions and rushed to the scene. They assumed we had shot and captured the third terrorist and that our chase was completed.

The wounded young man, serving in the southern Iran at Bandar Abbas Navy base, and was a cousin of the terrorist. He had come home for vacation and was getting ready to go duck hunting with his father. Later, the aunt told us, the terrorist was also at this house, and when all the officers ran to the door, he had jumped over the wall — vanished again.

Most of the villagers came around the house to see what the gunshot was about. They surrounded our cars. With two other officers, I moved the young soldier to my car, and one of the officers took a blanket and pushed on the wound area to prevent loss of too much blood. The villagers around our cars were seriously angry about the injury to the soldier and tried to prevent the car from leaving the village. They wanted to fight us. I fired a few shots into the air and shouted that I would shoot anyone who stayed in front of our car and blocked us from leaving. The mess of shooting young soldier and conflict with villager prevented me from organizing multiple chase teams for the third terrorists. My concern was to take the young soldier as soon as possible to Babol's hospital. Before leaving the village, I assigned 4 officers with a car to drive around the village for the third terrorist, and check the roads from village to Amol and Babol.

Finally, we rushed to the hospital, and I asked for an immediate operation to save the young soldier's life. The surgery was successful, and the soldier survived, but a problem surfaced — he was addicted to drugs. For the next few weeks, I asked a drug dealer to provide him the minimum amount of the drug he needed to survive. At first, the drug dealer was afraid and insisted that he had never sold any drug; but one of the local officers, who knew him, explained the situation and convinced him to cooperate. The soldier recovered fully and left for service to a Navy base within a month.

After the revolution, the third terrorist returned to Babol and became a local hero. The injured ones recovered and were convicted of murder of the young officer. However, they were freed when Khomeini's government took over Shah's government. After the revolution, in order to prevent prosecution, the officer who shot the soldier mistakenly, claimed that he had followed the order of his commanding officer. After this event, the situation worsened. I had to carry my revolver at all the times, and at night keep it close to my bed. Daily conflicts took place with demonstrations, in some cases, explosions and destruction of government and business properties. In addition to officers who were ready to fight and calm the city, we had tanks, jeeps, and soldiers, ready and anxious to clean the city from demonstrations and destruction.

Our orders from the federal government remained to not use force, that the government branches were in negotiations to end the national unrest peacefully. The head of opposition in my region was a medical doctor, Dr. Tahari. I knew him personally, and almost everybody in the force and city knew he is the leader of the opposition in this region. It would have been easy to eliminate this leader, which could weaken the opposition's plotting organization in the Babol and region, but we had to follow the federal government's orders.

10

Losing Two Great Men

During those days, most of my time was spent in the office and I barely could go

home to see Bahar and the children. When I slept at home, I slept with my revolver

under my pillow and the phone within close reach.

In the middle of the unrest, I was in my office one day and received a phone call

from Amol. My father had a heart attack and was admitted to the hospital. He was 63

years old and, fortunately, the heart attack happened while he was at work at the

hospital. I changed into civilian clothes and when I arrived at Amol Hospital, my

mother was sitting next to my father's bed. She was sad and very worried about my

father's condition and urged me to take care of him. I spoke with the doctor who told

me the heart attack was a serious one and that my father needed to remain in the

hospital for additional tests and close observation.

He could speak, and I spent a few hours with him, while my mother took a

break. We talked about my daily work, Bahar and children, and being in a dangerous

situations and my status as a target. I assured him that I could take care of myself, my

family, and my assignments. Before I left, my uncles and aunts with a few older cousins

came to the hospital to visit him. They assured me that they would stay with my mother and continue monitoring my father's progress. They knew I had so many problems in Babol and could not stay away from the city for too long. I left the hospital with feeling of hopelessness and sadness. After few hours, I went back to Babol with the uncertainty that what chaos could happen next, without any power to prevent it.

A few days later, I received a call from my mother-in-law that Bahar's father, who was 58 years old, had also a massive heart attack, and was transferred to the Sari Hospital. I got permission from the colonel to leave for Sari.

When Bahar and I reached the hospital, we were told Mr. Nasri died immediately following his heart attack. Dealing with the daily turmoil in the city and country, losing Bahar's father, and having my father in the hospital, our lives could not get much rougher.

Bahar had been very close to her father and they took many trips together around the country. She still shares the happy memories from those days. Bahar was devastated, and losing her father brought sadness, stress, and grief. But she knew what a tough situation we were in and she tried her best to hide her emotional pain from children and all of us.

A respectful burial for Mr. Nasri was held in Sari's cemetery. He was a great man who had made a lifelong commitment to take care of his family of nine, and to unconditionally support his children in advancing their education and lives. I loved and respected him dearly, and enjoyed conversations with him and being in his presence. He was generous, with a kind and handsome face, and is deeply in the hearts of his family and friends forever.

My father and Mr. Nasri were friends who once a while got together, and father complained that Mr. Nasri was not visiting him in the hospital at Amol. We never told him he'd died from a heart attack a few days earlier.

About a week after the funeral, after spending three days in headquarters without going home, I changed clothes and drove to the hospital in Amol to visit my father. When I arrived, my mother, as usual, was at his bedside. She said to me, "Son, you stay with your father while I go outside for a little fresh air."

My father and I talked. I knew that he had loved the most my younger brother, Bahman, who had left for Sweden a few years before. He said he missed Bahman too much. I promised my father that when he recovered, I would arrange his trip to Sweden to see Bahman.

As we talked, he had another heart attack. I rushed to the front desk and asked for help. A doctor and nurse rushed to my father's room, brought some equipment, and tried to bring him back. Meanwhile, my mother came back and was shocked to see the chaos, when a few minutes ago every sign had indicated my father's recovery and improvement.

After a short try, the doctor told us that my father had a massive heart attacked and died from it. I saw the fear and hopelessness in mother's face as she quietly cried. I spent a few hours with her and relatives at hospital.

The drive back to Babol was the toughest drive of my life. I was crying in my heart, but I knew he was watching me from heaven and was proud of me for not giving up in life. The rest of my life I have seen his serious face and heard his kind words in my heart and mind.

My father was a quiet, yet tough person. He had worked hard from the age of fourteen, and always tried his best to provide an acceptable living environment and opportunities for advancement in education and life for his seven children. He was respected by friends, family members, co-workers, and general public of the Shahi and Amol. He was proud of his children and their accomplishments. He loved Bahar, and always told me she was the best thing that happened in my life, and that I was lucky to have her as my wife. His serious face and strong voice have been a major motivation and source of energy for me to endure and overcome challenges in my life.

We arranged his burial in Amol's cemetery, the one most respected by the region's influential people and family members. My youngest brother who had just finished college moved in with my mother, which was a great relief for this tough

situation.

11

America's Beautiful Heart

With such uncertainty in our society, I wrote a letter to the central government requesting that they permit us to fight oppositions in our districts or release me from duties. I had heard that many other officers in charge around the country were requesting the same permission. Most of these officers in charge knew who the leaders were and how easily they could be eliminated; however, the central government and Shah were under pressure from the West to continue peaceful negotiations without a national bloodshed.

The problem with that approach was that the oppositions assumed negotiations were the sign of weakness, and they expanded the destructions and demonstrations, and the miscalculation by Shah and the government ended with a disastrous revolution for our beautiful and historic country. The situation worsened by the day. I continued to sleep with a revolver under my pillow, and each morning I was escorted with guards with machine guns to my office. The daily destructions continued. I felt ashamed by having soldiers, tanks, officers, and manpower at hand, and could only stand by and watch the burning and fighting without any forceful actions to prevent them.

My friend, Javad, was a doctoral student at Ball State University in Muncie, Indiana, USA. In summer 1978, he contacted and informed me that he was coming to Iran to visit his family and friends. I explained the social difficulties and turmoil that was started by oppositions to Shah, and after losing the two greatest men in my life — my father and my father-in-law —Bahar and I thought it might be good idea if Javad arranged an acceptance into graduate school for both of us at his university. He sent me acceptance for graduate work in Political Science at Ball State University, and language acceptance from Illinois University at Urbana Champaign. The university acceptance letter would not guarantee acceptance to the program until student finish the language course in accredited institution and pass the TOFEL (Test of English as a Foreign Language).

In late September, Javad came to Iran. His family talked with me to convince Javad to marry before returning to the United States. I had a good friend and colleague, Mr. Mahmoody, who had a very nice daughter, Maryam, who was a student in a local teacher college. Javad and Maryam met, they liked each other, and I recommended Javad as a kind and caring person to Maryam's family. In a few weeks, after spending a great deal of time together, they married, with the plan for Maryam to leave Iran and go to America with Javad.

During this time, daily demonstrations and distractions reached beyond control. Bahar and I made the decision to discuss with both sides of our families the possibility of leaving Iran and going to America. All family members were opposed to this decision. They reminded us that we had established great foundations in our financial, social, and professional lives in Iran, and they thought it would be too risky for us to start everything from scratch in a new country.

We reasoned that they could be right. We enjoyed a top-quality life. We had a young girl who played and took care of Sheila and Shadi, and an older woman who cleaned the house and helped in the preparation of meals. We also had a driver. In addition, Bahar and I had great jobs: I was a captain, had two degrees, distinguished services, was well-known in the region, and had a great chance to advance in the military as high as general by the age of forty-five. Bahar was teacher in high school and in a few years could be in charge of the school or the city education administration.

Meanwhile, I had a call from leader of the opposition, the doctor that I knew, who encouraged me to join the opposition for a bright future. My response was a short one: "Go to hell."

Bahar and I already had acceptances for graduate study at Ball State University and English course for passing TOFEL from University of Illinois. The most important and difficult part of the travel plan was to get student visas to America for our family of four. The American Embassy in Tehran was under pressure, with daily demonstrations, but the American Embassy in Tabriz was open, and the environment in the city of Tabriz was much calmer than in Tehran.

I travelled to Tabriz and took our acceptance letters from Ball State University and Illinois University with me. Upon arrival at the Embassy, I introduced myself as a captain in Shah's Army who needed support and help from the American Embassy. Usually, an appointment for a visa would take months, but the Embassy personnel was kind and arranged an immediate appointment for me with the ambassador. The ambassador knew the future could be extremely dangerous for officers and their families. He reviewed my acceptance letter. The Ball State University letter acceptance was valid; however, my language acceptance from Illinois University had expired. He was kind to advise me to contact my officer friends in secret services, who may have had some ideas about where and how I could get a language acceptance in a few days. "Come back for the visas as soon as you got the language acceptance," ambassador told me.

I returned to Tehran and contacted officer friends for help. In less than a day, they found an address of a boutique shop in northern Tehran where I could get a valid language acceptance letter from one of the universities in America. I went to the address, paid $150 for a language acceptance letter, and the store manager typed my

name in the blank space of a valid, signed language acceptance letter from Manchester

College, New Hampshire, United States. I realized that this language acceptance from

Manchester College might be a forged one and my name illegitimately was typed on the

acceptance letter. The end well justified my risk and the means of the action. All the

foreign embassies knew the emergency conditions in Iran and tried to be flexible about

those might be in danger and need help to leave Iran.

Two days later, I returned to the American Embassy in Tabriz. Ambassador was

informed that I came back with valid acceptance. The ambassador was about to have

lunch, but was kind to accept me. Ambassador said, "Would you like to join me for

lunch?" I replied, "Appreciate your kindness, I am in rush to return to Babol, and

request your visa approval." Ambassador said, "You know, you are 32 years old, many

years away from education." He continued, "With family of four, you are going to have

tough years in front of you in America." I said, "Yes I know, try my best to succeed." I

continued, "My hope is Iran would be backed to normal and I could return after

graduate work in America." Ambassador said, "I hope too." The ambassador

continued, "In case, at some point, you could not endure the new life, I would approve

a four-year visa with multiple entry to America for you and family." It was a great

generosity and futuristic thinking of the ambassador to issue this type of visa. This type of visa would enable my family and me to return back to Iran, and if the situation in Iran worsened, to go back to America without having to go through the visa process again.

The ambassador was a gentleman with a good heart and great kindness. I wish I could see him now to express my appreciation again, and to talk about our family's success stories and accomplishments in the United States.

After we made the decision to leave Iran for America, we put the house, which was 90 percent completed, on the market, and sold it much less than its real value. The buyer, a businessman and who I wrongly believed was a trusted businessman and a friend, paid a fourth of the price in cash, with the remainder to be paid with four checks over the following twelve months. I gave authority to my co-worker, Mr. Mahmoody, to cash the checks and send the money to me in USA. Unfortunately, the businessman buyer knew I could not return to Iran to collect the money myself, and he paid only one-third of the value of the four remaining payments, saying if I wanted his money I'd better come back and get it.

The turmoil and uncertainty surrounding us made it impossible to sell our other properties and personal belongings. We gave authority to family members to deal with all other properties and gave away almost all of our personal belongings to friends and to charities. We said goodbye to all of our family members and friends and told them our plan was to stay in America a few years to study; that after graduate work, we would return to Iran. Our hope was that in the next few years, the general public would come to understand that this is a wrong revolution.

My mother and Bahar's mother, who had recently lost their husbands, had the hardest time in accepting the fact we were leaving to go so far away to America.

When we were about to leave Babol for Tehran, our next-door neighbor said to us, "No one comes back to Iran from America after living there for a few years." She said she would not see us ever again.

12

Start of Adventure,

Chicken Chest or Chicken Breast

Our trip to Tehran and to the airport was a sad and anxious one. Seeing so much

destruction and foolishness made Bahar and me deeply depressed, and fearful for the

future of Iran, our family members, and the more than 90 percent of honorable Iranians

that deserved a prosperous and respected society. Leaving our country felt sad and

guilty, guilty for our mothers whom lost their husband and going to lose their children

and grandchildren, for brothers and sisters left behind in a turmoil condition. We knew

not much about American education, life, and society, but we felt we have adequate

experience to deal with unexpected and unanticipated future events. We also believed

we have strong reasons to leave our country for now and we pray for situation to be

able to return to our motherland.

We felt restless and uneasy on our trip to America. We knew that lack of

efficiency in English, having been away from education for years, and having limited

cash, would be primary and crucial challenges for us to deal with in the next few years.

Bahar and I barely knew English. Sheila was four years old and Shadi was less than two

years old; neither of them knew a single word in English.

After landing in Indianapolis, Javad rented an Oldsmobile and drove all of us to

Muncie, the home of Ball State University, a wonderful university with about 20,000 students, great faculty, staff, and a beautiful campus. In addition of Ball State, Muncie

was home of Ball Corporation and a few General Motors parts production factories. The

population was about 70,000 and it was about 40 miles northeast of Indianapolis.

We stayed at Javad's home for a week. It was a two-bedroom home, and the four

of us slept in one of the bedrooms. Javad helped us learn some of the basic shopping in

stores and how to deal with daily needed services. He gave us a tour of the city, the Ball

State University campus, and helped us open a bank account.

Iran, our great country with great civilization and culture in its history has had

the kindness and most caring people in the world. Iranian were famous in helping each

other, and having a humble, warm, and human society. The last twelve months

everybody was unhappy and had difficult time in life, work, and society. The future

was gloomy and uncertain for majority of the people and no one was sure of what

would happen from one day to the next. Smiles were rare and could see unhappy faces

everywhere.

When we went to Muncie Mall, we were so surprised to see people were happy

and smiling. Some politely said "Hi." We heard so many times the word "Sorry," when

somebody got close or blocked your way. The store managers rushed to greet you and offered help to find what you were looking. The people's gentleness and the community's kindness boosted our confidence and reduced our anxiety.

Javad introduced us to American football and explained the sport and rules to us when, for the first time, we went to a Ball State football game and did not understand what was going on. American football was unknown in Iran and most other countries outside of America, where soccer is called football and is by far the most popular sport in the world.

On our third day in Muncie, I went to the license bureau to get my driver's license in order to buy a car. I barely could speak and comprehend English. I took the written test, understanding some words in the sentences. A gentleman was taking the test next to me, and he asked me a question. I did not understand a word of it; I shook my head. He was not happy and thought I was snubbing him.

I answered multiple-choice questions by guessing and answered some of the traffic signs correctly. I had three errors — enough to pass the written test. When I went to take the driving test, the officer realized I did not understand his instructions and he asked for a translator. I asked my friend Javad to join us and officer accepted him as my translator. Javad sat in the back seat of the car and translated the officer's instructions in Farsi. I easily passed the driving test. The officer was surprised that I passed the written test, and he was entertained by Javad's translations of driving test commands in Farsi.

I was so proud that I successfully accomplished my first experiment in America and received my driving license. Bahar, too, was so surprised and proud. We were so happy. Even Sheila and Shadi became excited and laughed, not understanding what had happened.

The next day, Bahar and the children wanted fried chicken for dinner. Bahar and I carefully checked the Farsi to English translation dictionary and practiced what to ask when we ordered the dinner. We went to Ross Supermarket in Muncie and I asked the lady at the food counter for three chicken legs and three chicken chests. In the Farsi dictionary, breast referred to part of a woman's body, so we thought chest was the right word to use.

The woman had a difficult time understanding me and I had to repeat my order many times for the "three chicken chests." The lady behind the counter smiled and said, "Honey, you can say three chicken breasts."

I thought she might be tricking me, so I repeated, "No, I want three chicken chests."

She called another lady in the store over and told her, "Can you tell him it is not bad to say the word chicken *breast*."

I still refused to say chicken *breast* and they gave up, handed me a basket with three chicken legs and three chicken chests. Later, this became a popular story at gatherings with friends and our department in the university.

In the early years, our accents and lack of knowledge about American ingredients made it a difficult task to order foods, especially when using the drive-through for ordering the food. The Pizza Hut and Kentucky Fried Chicken were big winners, with all the family members. Even today, when my grandchildren asked, we stop by at the drive through to order foods, I ask them pull down the window and order whatever they like. Sometimes they take advantage of it and order much more than was planned.

Our college acceptance was from Ball State, but the language acceptance was from Manchester College in Manchester, New Hampshire. The acceptance letter, content, and signature were real, only my name was added in the blank space by the shop owner in Tehran. The reason for being a real acceptance letter was when I presented to Manchester College for registration, the registration office without any question validated the letter. I could not go to Ball State until I finished successfully my language course and pass the TOEFL, the foreign language test for foreign students with at least 500 points.

Our plan was to buy a car and to drive to New Hampshire. Javad and I went to a Chevrolet dealer in Muncie, and I selected a large, brown Nova, which was priced about $5,000. I had $6,000 cash in my pocket and gave $5,000, all in $100 bills, to the car dealer. He was surprised that I paid in cash and checked the $100 bills for counterfeit.

Javad told me most people pay large amounts with credit cards or cashier checks; rarely do people carry large amounts of cash. In Iran, almost all transactions, small or large, were by cash and people carried a large amount of cash all the time. In 1970s, credit cards were not available, and were not offered by the banks in Iran. Usually everyone carried cash for minor and major transactions.

After I bought the car, I went to the License Bureau of Muncie and paid for a license plate that I thought would be valid for as long as I owned the car. That was going to be another huge awakening.

Our family packed our few belongings into the car and with Javad and Maryam, we started a long, enlightening trip from the Midwest to the Northeast of the United States. It was a great opportunity to learn the American highway system, traffic rules, and driving etiquette, and we saw many beautiful sites during our long trip. It was amazing for us to see how a large and developed country America was. It was astonishing that every few miles you could stop by at gas stations, restaurants, fast foods, and see all these developed small and large cities on the way. We stopped by at a few of public parks (State and Federal). We ate and had short walk, while Sheila and Shadi were playing and running around. The allocations of those beautiful lands, rivers, mountains to public brought admiration and appreciations to those futuristic leaders

made these beautiful environments for generations to come.

After two days, we reached Manchester, a beautiful small town with great

people, in the far northeast of the United States. We rented a small house from a kind

Greek family, who had one high-school age daughter. We bought some basic kitchen

and sleeping needs, and a small TV. We all were excited that we have a place to call

home again.

I went to Manchester College, paid about a $1,000 tuition fee and registered for

the course, which was scheduled to start in a few days. In the second day at

Manchester, we all went to a sport store. The manager seemed happy to see us, kindly

offered us drinks, and said some nice words I barely understood. Javad talked with him

for a short time, and Javad started laughing.

When we left the store, Javad told me he thought you were the baseball player

from South America that recently joined the Boston Red Sox. I think my dark hair and

mustache made him believe I was that baseball player. After four days, Javad and

Maryam flew back to Muncie. Javad was a great help for our family in the new country.

It was the third week of November. The weather was turning cold and we

bought basic winter clothes. We had brought about $20,000 cash from Iran and had

already spent about a third of it. Bahar was in charge of our finances and kept us on track. Our landlord's daughter began teaching us to speak English. We watched TV and were happy to recognize and understand some of the words on the shows.

Finally, my English classes started, and I was excited about learning the language; but it was tough and very time consuming. Most of the students were very young, around eighteen years old, and from rich families from Middle East countries, with no timeline for passing TOFEL or to start college. These young students had little desire to study and pay attention in class. At thirty-two, I did not fit with this young group — I was the only student with a great obligation to learn English, pass TOEFL exam, and start graduate work as soon as possible, before we ran out of money.

After a week in the class, I called Javad and asked him to contact Illinois University to renew my expired acceptance of their English program. Javad was surprised and asked why I wanted to change. I explained the lack of the classmates' commitment to learn and slow progress of the class. The renewed acceptance letter might help me to convince the immigration officer in Boston to permit me to drop the language course in Manchester College, and start the course at Illinois University. Within the week, I received a current language acceptance letter from Illinois University, which indicated a new language course was scheduled to start after the first week of January.

I had only a few weeks to change universities. On a snowy and very cold day, the four of us drove from Manchester to the immigration office in Boston. In the 1970s, car insurance was optional in Iran, and I did not have car insurance for the first year in the America, and my car was back wheel drive. When I think back, it's pretty scary to think what could have happened in a new country, in winter on the snowy road of the Northeast and Midwest.

After a few hours waiting, a middle-aged lady, an immigration officer agreed to meet with me and listen to my request. I explained the situation at Manchester College, and how it was different for me because I had a family and limited finances, and I needed badly to go someplace where I could study and learn English in order to pass TOEFL. I explained that the first acceptance from Illinois University had expired, and I had just received a new one.

The immigration officer said, "You already registered at Manchester College, you have to finish the course here." I explained, "I appreciate her reconsideration of her decision." She said, "No, No." Meanwhile, Shadi, who was less than two years old, started to play and to talk with the officer with a few English words that she knew. Little Shadi had big, bright eyes and beautiful curly hair. She was playful and could easily warm up to any stranger. When I saw the officer begin playing with Shadi, I repeated my transfer request, "Please reconsider, and your decision might change our life for better." She hesitated a few seconds, then said," I will sign your transfer letter, never done before." She signed the transfer letter and gave it to me. We left her office with great joy, and we knew Shadi was the main reason that immigration officer approved my transfer to the University of Illinois.

The next day, I informed Manchester College that I had received permission to transfer to Illinois University. I also informed our good landlord of the transfer, and he graciously terminated the rental agreement. We packed our few things, including the TV, and placed them in the trunk of our big Nova car. We bought an America Road map (a road Atlas) and Bahar was in the charge of navigating, while our two beautiful daughters sat in the back seat and played.

We started driving early morning; the weather was cold, and some roads were covered with snow. It was fun for all of us to stop at fast food restaurants, in a few minutes get the foods, eat in the car and drive away. A few times, we made wrong turns and got lost, but by 11:00 that night, we reached Cleveland, Ohio. We all were tired and hungry.

I tried to find a place to eat but got lost and ended up in the wrong part of the city of the Cleveland. I saw several young men gathered around a fire on the corner of the street. I stopped the car, got out, and with my deep accent and barely able to speak English, I asked, "Sir, I am lost. How could I get back to the highway?"

The young men were shocked. They looked at me as though I was from another planet. They laughed and looked at the car and saw Bahar and the children. One of them came closer, talked loudly, and used his hands to show directions. I guessed he was telling me, "*You are in the wrong and dangerous place of the city. Drive fast on this road then turn right; after a while you will see I-90 … make sure you do not stop any place, under any condition, until you reach I-90.*" I barely understood what he was saying, but I got an adequate idea from his hand movements and understanding some of the words.

We returned to I-90. A few miles later we found a gas station, bought gas and some food, and continued our drive to Indiana. By the following afternoon, we reached Javad's home in Muncie and spent a few days with Javad and Maryam in Muncie.

In the first week of December 1978, we drove from Muncie to Illinois University in Urbana Champaign, Illinois. I went to the Foreign Student Department, gave them my acceptance to study language, paid another $1,000.00 for tuition, completed an application for student housing, and we moved into a two-bedroom student-housing apartment on the campus. The weather was extremely cold and most of the roads were icy, making walking and driving very difficult. We tried hard to learn how to survive the cold and icy weather and I still did not know I needed to have car insurance.

The apartment was so small in comparison to where we had lived in Iran. Student life and classes were so much different from Manchester University, there was high demands for excellence in assignments and all students worked hard to succeed. In comparison to be a captain in charge of a city and a few serve you at all the time, it was a 360-degree changes in my and my family's life. The classes were tough and expectations of the university for the foreign students were very high. I had to study harder than all the young students in order to catch up with them on assignments.

There was a nice and helpful family, Soofi, from Iran. The husband was a doctoral student and they had two beautiful daughters who became friends with Sheila and Shadi. The wife, Shahin was kind and helped us to adjust to our new life in this university, city, and America.

Foreign students needed a score of 500 on the TOEFL in order to be considered for acceptance into a good university. After the second month, our English class took a practice test. My score was a very disappointing 430. I worried that I would not be able to get the over 500 score by end of the semester. In a month later, in our second practice test, I had a score of 475, which was an improvement, but still not adequate. After each practice test, I increased my daily hours of study and in some days, I studied over 10 hours in the University's Library.

Meanwhile, Bahar's mom came to America to visit Bahar's brother, Ali, who was a student at Fresno State University, California. After a month in Fresno, she came to see us at Urbana, which was a great morale booster for all of us. Having her with us was a blessing and helped me to focus even more on preparation for final TOEFL test. Sheila was just over four years old, and we registered her at the university daycare center to be with other children and learn English. Kids pick up on language fast and she made great advances by being at daycare and playing with the children.

At the end of the semester, I took the real TOEFL test and my score was 507, which was enough to be accepted to the graduate program at Ball State University. This was a great first success in our educational life in the United States. After a few weeks, Bahar's mom left for Iran and we started preparations to move to Ball State University in Muncie, Indiana. We had a few days of the free times, we visited the beautiful city of Chicago. Our best memory was we went to Rigley field, watched the Chicago Cubs baseball game. In addition of the game, the number of people in the Rigley field, the drinking beers, and eating food were a major entertainment for us. In summer 1979, we packed our few belongings in the car, and drove to Muncie — the first American city we called home for ever.

13

Student Life, License Plate and Jail,

Call from Amir, Officer Escaped to Russia

Iranian 1979 revolution terminated the reign of Mohammad Reza Shah Pahlavi

who was supported by America and west. The revolution overthrow Pahlavi Dynasty,

which was the last of over 2,500 years of continuous Persian Monarchy in the world.

The Pahlavi Dynasty was replaced by Islamic Republic under Ayatollah Ruhollah

Khomeini the leader of revolution. The revolution was supported by various Islamist

and leftist organizations. Shah left Iran on January 16, 1979 and Khomeini returned to

Iran on February 1, 1979. To control the different branches of government and society,

many government influential leaders and military leaders were executed. The cleanup

claim and execution even reached to most cities, targeted some lower rank officers and

officials who carried assignments and orders before revolution. As I heard from my

friends in Iran, one of my officer (driver), Kalige was executed, and a second lieutenant

who in the last few months before revolution was reporting to me also was executed.

The first few months of the revolution, news of the mass executions of the Shah's

supporters were a grave indication of not being able to return to Iran and losing

homeland forever by Iranian who left Iran during revolution.

With the new government in place in Iran, I could not see any way we'd be able to return in the near future.

I was accepted to Ball State for Political Science, but that graduate degree would not be marketable for an immigrant in a new country. In the late 1970's, Computer science, however, was a new field and was becoming popular worldwide, particularly in the United States, and there was much potential for getting a job after graduation. Some universities, including Ball State, had just started to offer undergraduate and graduate degrees in this new field.

My friend, Javad, Bahar and I thought that, with my math background, it might make sense for me to switch my graduate study to Computer Science. Bahar and I knew that as I had never worked with or even seen a computer, it was going to be a tall task to seek graduate degree in this field. Together we decided that Bahar would delay her graduate work to give me plenty of time to endure a tough two years of the graduate work. We both firmly believed that our future survival and prosperity started with my success in earning this degree.

From the 1950s to the 1970s, watching American movies were the most exciting events for young people around the world. When I was in elementary school, I paid one cent and sat on the ground or on the bench right in front of the cinema's big screen.

165

With deep excitement, I watched the American movies, and could repeat to friends and family, minute by minute, the events and actions from the movies. My wish was someday to visit America. TV did not exist, and radio programs were rare. At breakfast, there may be a 10-minute radio broadcast children story, which all the children anxiously waited to hear to discuss it at school.

Iranian children grew up with American movies, especially Westerns. Burt Lancaster, John Wayne, Kirk Douglas, Charlton Huston, Paul Newman, Gary Cooper, Susan Hayward, and Natalie Wood… these stars were a major part of our childhood and shaping who we became as adults. The characters in these movies were strong, confident, and achievers in very tough environment and situations. In addition of families' demands and growing in tough conditions, these achiever characters taught us never gave up and be resilience in any condition.

In July 1979, Javad and I went to see the Chair of Computer Science, Dr. Clinton Fueling. He was a few years older than I was at the time, around thirty-seven, and he reminded me of Burt Lancaster.

Javad introduced me to Dr. Fueling as a captain in Shah's army, and who needed a chance to start a new professional life in the America. I explained that my math and undergraduate work prepared me to learn and succeed in this new field, Computer Science.

I also explained that with a family of four, no financial support, and little hope to be able to return to Iran, I needed badly to study Computer Science in order to have a better chance to find a job in America.

Dr. Fueling was not convinced that I was ready for the program, considering I had not even seen a computer before, and my English was not strong enough to understand everything in the classrooms. Dr. Fueling said, "The subject is new and popular." He continued, "There are many applicants mostly in their early twenty." I said, "I am asking for an opportunity, even if possible, a conditional for only one semester." I continued, "My age and life experience could help me to succeed." Dr. Fueling smiled and said, "I know you have many reasons to work hard in your courses."

Ultimately, Dr. Fueling accepted my promise that I would study hard to succeed. He trusted that my life experiences, and the conditions I had faced and overcome in Iran, would ensure that I would work hard and do well in the program. He approved my acceptance with the condition that he would review my advancements for a final decision after the fall semester.

The advisor of the graduate program mapped my courses for the next two years. I started from the beginning, taking three courses — Basic, FORTRAN, and Assembler1

— for the first semester. Dr. Fueling gave me permission to sit in the summer classes for the next three weeks to gain understanding of computer expressions, assignments, and teachers' expectations.

That now squared away, I had another important lesson to learn. This time having to do with the United States and how car registration worked over here. In Iran, license plates are a one-time purchase you make when you buy your car and you don't have to worry about it again. I didn't realize when we bought our Chevy Nova and I got the plates that they would expire in six months. I did not know anything about the American registration expiration and renewal processes for the cars.

It was fall 1979, I just started my first semester in the computer science and became a graduate student in the Computer Science Department. One evening after class, I was driving with my family near the Muncie Mall, which is in the middle of the city. An officer pulled me over and asked me to come out of the car to look at my license plate. "What is this?" he asked, pointing to the plate.

I thought maybe the plate was dirty, so I cleaned it with my hand. "Is it okay now?" I asked him.

He got a little mad and forcefully said, "No."

The plate was a little bent from all the snow and ice in Illinois, so I thought his dissatisfaction was with the shape of the plate. I tried to straighten it as much as possible with my hands. I saw that the officer was becoming very angry and he was

touching his handgun. I thought he was going to arrest me for violation that I did not

know what it was. He said, "Give me your registration and driver license."

He checked my registration and driver's license, wrote a ticket, gave it to me

without saying another word, and drove away. Bahar and I were relieved that the

matter ended peacefully. I looked at the ticket, and it indicated I should go to a court

office and pay the fine of about sixty dollars.

At school, one of my classmates checked the ticket and explained the obligation of the

annual renewal of registration and changing the sign on the license plates. The next

day, I went to the Muncie DMV and renewed my registration and license plate.

Then, on the date indicated on the ticket as the due date, I went to the court office

in Muncie and presented my ticket with cash, but the clerk told me the ticket was

written for the court in Albany. She was not sure why the ticket was written for the

court in Albany. She advised me to go there the next day to pay my fine at that court.

I did not know where Albany was, but I learned it was about fifteen miles from

Muncie and arrived there around 2:00 the next afternoon, it was a small town. The court

was a small room over a shop in the middle of downtown Albany. The court was

closed, but a clerk was there and ready to leave. I said, "Hi, could you please help me

with this ticket?" Clerk smiled and said, "Court is closed." I think she was entertained with my deep accent and measured talking. I said, "I came from Muncie and I am new to this area." She asked to see my ticket, I gave my ticket to her. She said, "it past due date." And continues, "Address is in Muncie, why officer sent you here." I replied, "I don't know, and officer did not say anything." She tried to help, said, "We send you a new notice with new date to come back." She continued, "Judge will make a decision about your fine." I said, "Appreciate your help." She said," Do not worry about delay and ticket."

Two months passed, and I did not receive any notice from court of the Albany, and I forgot the fine. Meanwhile, I heard that after the revolution, many of the Shah's oppositions, including those three terrorists that killed officer and were subject of the 12 hours chase had returned and were in key power positions.

Most of the Computer Science faculty members knew about my past in Iran and being captain in the Shah's forces, and were aware of rough treatment of the military officers and Shah's supporters by the revolutionary government. One day, in the middle of my Assembler1 class, two police officers came to class and asked my professor, "Who is Sam Navadar?" The professor became worried and asked the officers to wait outside until class was over. The professor was very surprised and asked me, "Do you know why they are here?" I said "No." He said, "So strange, we never had situation officer interrupt class." I said, "I can go with them now." Professor said, "No, do you want I ask them why they asked for you?" I said, "No, I prefer to go now, not later in recess." Professor said, "Are you sure, do you want I tell the office and Dr. Fueling?" I said, "Thanks, please after I left tell Dr. Fueling." I thought if I waited after class, then the whole department would see me arrested by two officers, and many stories could be fluctuating among the students.

I came out of the class and informed them that I was Sam Navadar. They took me to the local police station, a small station with a few individual cells in downtown Muncie. I sat in the room with a few officers and emptied my pockets. They asked me some personal questions and when they found out I was captain in Shah's force, and for years was in charge of a state prison, they tried to make me comfortable and offered me a chair in the office, not lock me in a cell.

I asked them, "Can I look around?" One of the officers asked, "Why, you want a tour?" I said, "I can compare with what we had in Iran, and this could bring a lot of memories." They laughed and one of them walked with me around and explained their operations. It was interesting to see it and to compare with what I managed in Iran.

One of the officers explained that I did not go to Albany court for my license plates fine, so the judge issued a warrant for my arrest, and that I must pay a $1,000 bond to be free. The judge also issued a new date for me to go to Albany court for my violation. I called Bahar, explained briefly the situation, she went to bank and came with $1,000 cash to pay the bond. The next day, Dr. Fueling, came to see me after class,

he asked what the story was. I explained the event, he offered his personal or

university's help. I appreciated and told him the matter is a simple misunderstanding

and would be solved with no trouble.

A few days later, on the new court appearance date, I went back to Albany. The

judge was not happy with my delay in the paying the fine and asked for my

explanation of the violations and delay. I told him the whole story including my arrest

from the classroom. He was an old and kind man, who shook his head throughout my

explanations, and seemed angry. The judge said he was ashamed of everything that had

happened to me for a simple license plate misunderstanding, and of the zero attempts

by all involved to help. He shook my hand, fined me only $1.00, and closed the file.

The story became an amusing anecdote in the Computer Science Department and

also among friends and family over the years.

I wrote the following event in the chapter 6 for undoing the mystery of the

Amir's escape and give readers the whole story at one chapter. I repeated a brief of

Amir's phone call to fit with the sequence of the time and condition of my living in the

America.

In spring of 1980, I received a long-distance call. When I heard the voice on the

other end of the line, I could not believe it. It was Amir Hossain Ahmadian, the officer

172

who escaped with two prisoners many years ago from our prison in Sari, Iran. The escape chapter contains some of the missing information that Amir shared with me in this phone call.

Amir and I talked for about an hour. He began the conversation by saying how deeply sorry he was to put me and other friends in difficult situations, and then explained the events that had taken place before and after the escape. Much of the information he shared had been a mystery, even to the investigating authorities. After hearing his side of the event, I could be the only one knew the whole story from both sides.

He told me that he'd hid for about ten days in Tehran, until his plan of the transfer to Russia became ready. His main training was in Russia and East Germany. Amir said he came back frequently to Iran with assignments to cause damage to the government or to assassinate influential leadership. Each time, after he completed his assignment, he'd go back into hiding in Lebanon or Palestine. He asked, "Sam, did you receive the letter I sent to you before leaving Iran?" He continued, "I sent to your brother in Behshar, not direct to you." I replied, "No I did not read the letter, but my brother shared the content with me." He said, "I wanted to make sure to say sorry and good bye." I laughed, and said, "Do not worry, we both are perusing a new life." We also talked about our families in Iran.

After the revolution, Amir returned to Iran as a hero. He wrote a book and was asked to speak in universities and at national events. He said Khomani promised to let the people of Iran run the country, and not religion, but his supporters stole the revolution, took over all phases of governing the country, and pressured and created tension for the Fadaian Khalgh, who were the primary fighters in the revolution. Amir said Fadaian Khalgh members were ready to go underground and to start their new adventure with the Khomani's government.

Amir wished me the best and hoped that someday, in some place, we would see each other. I explained that I could not return to Iran and looked forward to a long-term stay in America. This was the last contact I had from Amir. I think he went underground and finally left Iran.

Later, in 1990, when with my family went to Sweden to visit my brothers and their families, my younger brother, Bahman, told me that he had heard Amir was in Sweden, and suggested we try to connect with him. I rejected the idea, thinking it would be too dangerous, to have anything to do with a man might be wanted by the Iranian government, and might also be wanted by some other active international groups.

In the late 1970s and early 1980s, computer science was taught on mainframe computers with card readers in the computer center's machine room. We inserted cards in a card puncher in the computer lab, typed our programs, and a card puncher made holes in the card. A new card was used for each line. When all lines of a program were punched, you would take the punched cards to the machine room window and hand them to the operator in charge, who registered them with your name.

The operator fed the cards into a mainframe that read them, compiled the program, executed it, and printed the program list and results of the execution on paper. Even one wrong word or number resulted in a major problem for a programmer, because a new card had to be punched to correct mistakes and the whole process had to be repeated through operator.

The first time I went to the computer lab to do my assignment, I stopped in front of a card puncher machine and looked at it for about fifteen minutes. One of my classmates, a young girl from Egypt, asked me if I needed help. I told her I did not know how to work with the punching machine and thanked her for her offer. She showed me where to type my user ID and password, and how to start the machine. She also explained where to take the cards and how to get printout. It was a kindness that was a great help for me and I always appreciated her help.

Surviving the first semester in Computer Science was, for me, even tougher than having over 1,000 prisoners in Iran. I was even too embarrassed to talk with Bahar about how hard the study and courses were. Those days only the Computer Science students used the computer lab, and most of them share ideas and help each other in the writing programs. I was much older than all of my classmates and was embarrassed to ask the young classmates for explanations about the assignments, programs, and chapters.

The first semester, I received an A in Basic and an A in FORTRAN, but a C in the Assembler1 course. Having a C grade in the graduate study program was not acceptable, especially since I had been accepted conditionally into the program. I had a meeting with Dr. Fueling to evaluate my performance and make a final decision about my acceptance into the graduate program.

Dr. Fueling told me he was satisfied with my efforts in the three courses, despite the C in Assembler1. He said he was sure it had more to do with my lack of fully understanding the English language than it did with not putting in the effort. He told me keep working hard, you will succeed in the program and will be graduated on time. He approved my acceptance into the computer science graduate program and told me to repeat the Assembler1 course.

176

I succeeded in passing the rest of the graduate program, earning "A" s in most of the courses. Over the two-year program, there were many days I had to spend over 15 hours in the library studying in order to catch up with the assignments. I used a Persian dictionary to comprehend the sentences, pages, and chapters in the textbooks. But computer science languages, terminology, and definitions were new, and most could not be found in the Persian dictionary. In some cases, I sought out some of my younger classmates in the library or lab and asked them to explain some of the concepts that I could not translate.

The Assembler2 (Machine Language) was a very difficult course, and I did well in this course. The teacher, Dr. Brown, even recommended weaker students to seek my help in the assignments, which gave me confidence that I was on the right track in this field. My mastery of Assembler2 was soon to lead to more exciting opportunities in the Computer Science Department.

14

Ball State's Kind Heart,

Employment and Deportation from America

Bahar was doing an unbelievable job with Sheila and Shadi in learning the American way of life, education, and the English language. Sheila started kindergarten at Mitchell School, a great school close to our student housing apartment in the university complex. Both daughters learned to speak English, without an accent, and loved playing with other children in our apartment complex playground. Sheila and Shadi showed so much intelligence in learning, which made us proud and very optimistic about their future.

Bahar had sacrificed and delayed her formal education until after I finished mine and started a job. While we brought in adequate money for the first year, we spent almost all of it on the car, tuition fees, rent, and food. We tried hard to cut expenses where possible. Bahar knew how to sew and made some of the kids' clothes; and instead of buying new clothes for herself, she wore what she had brought from Iran. I remember buying a pair of shoes for $2.00 and a shirt for $1.00 from Goodwill and wearing them for most of the year.

In 1980, it was so difficult to receive money from Iran, we could barely get any of the money we'd made from selling our properties. If we received a check from Iran, the maximum amount was $1,000, while my tuition for semester was even more than the received check. The received check from Iran had to be certified by a central bank in United States before it cleared, which could take additional two weeks.

America has the most wonderful and helpful people in the world — you do not know how great Americans are until you have lived someplace else. From time to time, we were late for tuitions or rent payments. We explained our situation, how the checks we'd received were in the process of being certified. In all situations, the people in charge did the best they could to help us, by extending due dates and delaying our payments.

In summer of 1980, before I started the second year of my graduate work, I applied for Graduate Assistantship for Computer Services in Research Computing at the Ball State University. Student with graduate assistantship would receive about $500 monthly, would pay almost nothing toward tuition, and would have the opportunity of hands-on experiences, which was a valuable asset for future employment.

I interviewed with Mrs. Jean Hamori, head of Research Computing, who was a leader with great experience and knowledge. Her husband was faculty and came as an immigrant from Eastern Europe. She was curious about my journey and thought it was fair to award me the graduate assistantship, and opportunity to work under her supervision as a graduate assistant.

This was a major break in our family's life and future successes. The learning was invaluable, free tuition was great, and $500 monthly was enough to cover our rent of $220 and our monthly food. Weekly, I worked 20 hours at Research Computing and attended my three computer classes.

Bahar was accepted into the Business Education graduate Program at Ball State University. She started her nightly courses, and during the days, continued to take care of our children and home. Sometimes she had to take the kids with her to the library to complete her assignments.

Those four to five years were the most important years of our life — as a family, we had a mission to work hard, not give up no matter what the situations were, and to mount paths for a good future for all four family members.

When I graduated in May 1981, computer science was rapidly coming in high demand. There were not many college graduates in computer science, and almost every company and institution needed to hire computer science graduates. Before any interview, with my friend Javad, we went to Purdue University, which had top doctoral program in Computer Science. The chairman of Computer Science was kind to see us and I explained the desire to be a PHD student at Purdue University. I also explained my financial reservation and asked for a fellowship award in order to cover tuition and some of the expenses. The chairman explained that all department fellowship already

180

was awarded for the coming year, and if I was accepted to the doctoral program, he

would consider me for the next year award. I appreciated his kindness and knew

financially, no way I could endure a year without fellowship award where I had no

other financial support.

Many of the companies came to the campus for interviews and my name was

forwarded, along with other graduated students, to the visiting companies. Almost all

candidates were well-qualified, twenty-one to twenty-three-year-old Americans;

whereas, I was thirty-five, with a deep accent, a big, dark mustache, and wore a dark

suit that I had brought from Iran. I participated in many campus interviews but did not

get any offers as summer came close to an end. My graduate assistantship had finished,

and there would be no more financial support of $500 monthly from the university. I

was desperate for a job to finance our rent and basic expenses. I was not bitter with lack

of success in the interviews. I believed that the younger candidates were better suited in

the long run for the companies and deserved to be hired, but I also needed a job. It was

easy to lose faith and beaten down with the lack of success in the interviews and blame

companies and this beautiful country. I knew if I started blaming then I would lose

optimism and faith that were our strength to succeed until this point. How in the world

I can blame, when I already blessed with so much kindness, help, and assistant from government officials such as ambassador in Iran, university officials such as Dr. Fueling and Mrs. Hamori, and numerous classmates and neighbors.

When I was graduate assistant, one employee in the department, David, knew I had many interviews without any success. He encouraged me to continue my search and not give up. One day, he called me at home and mentioned there was a position in Administration Computing at the Ball State University and encouraged me to apply. I went to the human resources department and applied for the position, with positive recommendations from the individuals in the research computing department.

After two interviews, I was told that if I were selected for the job, someone from human resources would contact me. Bahar and I were anxious as we waited day after day for word. Finally, after two weeks, I received an offer for the programmer job at a salary of $14,000 annually. This was another great break in our family's life. I gleefully accepted the offer and headed to human resources the following day to fill out the official hiring forms. When asked for my social security number, I told them I didn't have one, and they directed me to social security office downtown, and the office issued a social security card for me.

I started a week later, working with COBOL programming language, IMS and CICS IBM mainframe database and interface systems. Dr. Vebrougie, who had come from IBM, had a PhD in Computer Science, and was a pioneer in the use of computer applications in education, was appointed as head of Research Computing, and he recognized the campus needed to have Academic Computing for the support of the use of computers in education and worked closely with faculty members. He expanded the Research Computing assignments, included computers in the education section, and changed the name of Research Computing to Academic Computing.

I was in my third months in my new job when Dr. Vebrougie talked with Dr. Kramer, head of the Computing Services, about moving me to the new Academic Computing section to work with faculty and students. I was offered an $18,000 annual salary, which was a $4,000 raise within just a few months. I was delighted for the opportunity to work more closely with faculty members, and the new assignment was similar to what I had been doing as a graduate assistant.

Meanwhile, the Professor who taught Assember2 was retired, Dr. Fueling asked me to be an adjunct professor to teach Assembler2, in the Computer Science Department, which paid $2,500 for each course. It was a great happiness and comfort for our family to be making over $20,000 annually, and to have a solid job at the university, while a few months ago everything looked uncertain and gloomy.

In less than a year, Dr. Vebrougie created a new division, Instructional Computing, which he asked me to lead. I now had a staff of four and my salary jumped to $25,000 annually, which made us believe in a much stronger future and America as land of opportunity.

My team's assignments were to help faculty members in using computer applications in teaching and learning. Only a few universities in America managed a team of experts to develop hands-on applications in the form of simulations and case studies on the mainframe for learning and labs assignments.

My team's primary assignment was to work with experts and teachers to develop computer case studies and simulations for the interactive, hands-on practices and course activities for departments and colleges.

Dr. Hudson, in the School of Nursing, was the first faculty member who valued the enormous potential of computer case studies and simulations in advancing nursing education. For the next 15 years, we continued our collaborations in this journey and created many hands-on learning and artificial intelligent systems for nursing education at Ball State University.

Meanwhile, Bahar was a second-year graduate student. We still were living in the university's student housing, and had wonderful neighbors, the Chambanda family from Nigeria--a wife and husband with five children, including two the same ages as Sheila and Shadi. We saw our neighbors almost every day, and we enjoyed our conversations and shared our journeys to the new country. Our children became friends with each other, and they enjoyed playing together.

When I was teaching computer course for the department of computer science, I had two interesting students in my tough Assembler2 class: the girl from Egypt, who had helped me on my first day in computer lab; and our neighbor, Josef Chambanda. After class on the first day of my teaching, the girl from Egypt asked me how in the world did I finish my degree and become her teacher in such a short time. We laughed about it and I offered my help for the assignments. Assembler2 was Jose's last graduate course, and Josef had a hard time with it. I arranged private lessons for him at home and helped him to pass his last course.

Josef did great on the final exam, graduated with a master's degree and was hired by Ball Corporation as a programmer. His wife later graduated as a nurse, and all children succeeded in higher education. Our families continued to be friends until they moved with the Ball Corporation to Denver.

The Chambanda family, and my family, are a clear display of the greatness of America and its vast resources for advancement for all who work hard. This great country provided so much opportunity to succeed, even as immigrants with nothing to start with and having so many disadvantages at the start of their journey. My heart aches when I see or hear people blame this great country for their failures, and not themselves.

My working permission "H" visa was for two years, and the University Foreign Student Department worked with Computing Services, Computer Science, and me, to extend my work at the university as a teacher and Instructional Computing Leader.

In the middle of the spring semester, I was called to Dr. Kramer's office. He was the head of the both Administrative and Academic Computing and told me that he had received a letter from the Indianapolis Immigration Office stating that I did not have permission to work and teach at the university, and that he must immediately terminate my employment.

Dr. Fueling and Dr. Kramer were astonished with the letter, considering that in the last few months, all news from the University's Department of Foreign Students indicated that all paperwork was completed for my continuation at the university. Dr. Kramer asked Dr. Vebrougie to lead the activities related to this unexpected matter.

Dr. Vebrougie and I went to the office of the Head of Foreign Student Department, Mr. Robey. He brought my file and we reviewed all the prepared documents that had been submitted to the immigration office in Indianapolis. After reviewing the documents, we discovered that Mr. Robey, by mistake, sent half of my documents to Immigration Office in Hammond, Indiana, and the other half to Indianapolis office. Neither office had the full documentation needed to make the decision. The Indianapolis office issued my employment termination and ordered I report to the Immigration Office within a week.

Dr. Vebrougie reported to the vice president of the university that I did not have any fault in this matter, and that it was the university made mistake and should be responsible. To help me, the vice president and Dr. Kramer asked Dr. Vebrougie to travel with me to the Indianapolis Immigration Office and clarify the entire story to the officers in charge of my visa, and explain university's wish for combining the two parts of documents in Hammond and Indianapolis for a new decision in the matter.

After one hour of waiting at the immigration office in Indianapolis, Dr. Vebrougie and I met with two immigration officers. Without any explanation, one of them started screaming at me and angrily said that I was done with the university and must be deported from the United States. Dr. Vebrougie and I were astonished and confused by the officer's behavior and conduct.

I was furious about the way they were speaking to us. "You may have the right to scream at me, but you do not have the right to disrespect this gentleman, who is an American, has a doctoral degree, and has been sent by the university to explain this mistaken situation." The officer ignored my comment and was shaking his head, continue his remarks about my fault in providing all the needed documents.

Dr. Vebrougie was also shocked and very unhappy with the bad treatment. "This is the university's fault. Please be patient." The other office said you are done, no more discussion, your deportation letter is ready for you.

They made final decision before they hear what the situation was. The officer gave me my deportation notice, which indicated that in twenty-one days my family and I must exit the United States, from New York.

Upon our return, Dr. Vebrougie wrote a long report about the incident to vice president of the university. In brief, it included content such as, if he had not been with me, they might arrest me, and how he was ashamed how badly they treated an educated person who did not do anything wrong. He advised the university to do whatever is necessary to find a fair solution to this embarrassing situation.

Meanwhile, Bahar and I were evaluating our options and we were approaching fast to the deportation date. After a few years of uncertainty, gloomy future, financial misery, and hard work, our family just started to be in a solider ground to make some future plan with some level of certainty. It was too dangerous to go back to Iran, and with the short time we had, we could not find another country to go. Not to mention that we did not have enough money to survive for long without a job. We knew our resilience would be tested one more time, but with two young children the deportation and no place to go created tense and anxious days for us. Bahar and I thought our only

option could be to contact a few European countries' embassies to explain our situation

and ask for visa to their country and if possible, work permission. University already

done so much for us, we accepted the termination without complaining and blaming

university. Our gratefulness of what university have done for us in the last three years

was a motive that university communities all were trying hard to help us with this

unexpected difficult matter.

After a week of evaluation of all possible options and discussion, the university,

Bahar, and I decided for me to apply for political asylum in the United States. We

believed that my position as a captain in Shah's Force could be sufficient to be granted a

political asylum.

Having only ten days left until deportation, the university contacted Rep. Philip

Sharp in Washington D.C., from Delaware County, who was also a professor of Political

Science at Ball State University. Dr. Sharp offered to be personally involved in D.C. in

the processes of acquiring asylum. A few days before deportation date, I received the

official acceptance Letter of Political Asylum, which entitled my family and me to stay

and work in United States, without limitation of time and place. Our life returned to

normal again.

When I taught classes the first few sessions, I noticed all the students were leaning forward on the chairs. A sign that the students may have had a problem understanding my accent. I tried to write more on the blackboard and repeated more than usual each discussion items. After few sessions, I noticed that all students started to look more relaxed on their chairs, which was good sign that they had gotten used to my accent. My accent was a case of curiosity for some of the students in my class and in a few instants, students asked, "Where are you from, professor?" In a serious voice I responded, "From Texas." They knew I was not serious and might kidding but did not dare to repeat their question. Claiming to be from Texas became known among colleagues at the university and for fun sometimes at the meetings I was introduced as a Texan. The reason I told them from Texas came from, the western (Texan) movies I saw as child in Iran.

In the summer 1983, I received an early morning phone call from a friend telling me to read the Muncie daily newspaper. I bought the newspaper from a nearby grocery store. On the first page, I saw a list of twenty faculty and staff members who had received an extraordinary salary increase by Ball State University Board of Trustees based on their performance in the previous year. My name was at the top of the list with the highest percentage, an increase of 39.5 percent of my current annual salary. It was an exceptional achievement for me, and for my department, to be recognized by the university and rewarded this much-needed financial incentive in the annual raise.

In the fall of 1983, Bahar completed her degree in administration from Teacher College. In addition, Bahar had also taken some courses in Computer Science and programming languages from Computer Science department.

Sheila and Shadi were growing fast, and Sheila was a responsible, great child, who was very focused on education and sports. She started second grade at Mitchell School, where she was already top student in her class. Shadi was curious, full of energy, outgoing, and like her sister, very smart and good athlete. She started kindergarten at Mitchell School that fall. Mitchell School was about 300 yards away from our apartment. I loved to involve the kids in team sports to learn teamwork, respect, find new friends, improve their physical and social development. Our family first experience with American sport was baseball. Sheila was 9 years old, we registered her in the summer baseball league at the Mitchell Elementary School. We did not know anything about baseball, and we learned basic from our neighbor that her 10 years old son was playing in the little league. We bought the basic baseball gears for Sheila and took her to the practice. The families of the players were kind, supportive of coach, and cheerful all the time. I watched carefully what coach was teaching and at free times we went to a church close to the apartment, which had a good size grass field for extra practices.

When we had the first game, I saw the other side of the families, they yelled at the kids what to do, argued with coach about the positions their kids should play, and screamed at umpires in each call of strike or ball. I did not understand why around the bases were so much important for parents, they argued with coach about their kids to play on the first, second, third bases and short stop. I did not know why nobody liked their kids play outfield. I saw even parent pulled his son out of the game when coach took him from third base to outfield. Sheila played all the time outfield and we all were very happy with her position on the field.

I think the youth sport is for kids' physical, mental, and social development, kids enjoy the participation and activities, but unrealistic expectations by parents make it challenging for all involve in the youth sport including the kids. I remember a great statement from director of the State of Washington Elite Soccer Player Development program. My older grandson was invited to tryout, at the start of the tryout, the Director gathered all the parents and told them enjoy the few days tryout, appreciate and be satisfied your sons invited to tryout, remember none of them will be a professional player or will play in national team, some might play in college, lower your expectations and do not pressure your kids, create great and fun memories with your kids and sports. I wish all parents at all the time remember these two lines.

A few times in the youth soccer game at Gig Harbor, we did not have referee for the game and I was asked to referee the game. To prevent comments and screams by parents during the game, I went to the parents side of the field and told both teams' parents that I am 70 years old, your grandfathers' age, I have doctoral degree and retired from university, I am doing it as favor and volunteer, the only think I expect to hear from you is to tell the kids good job, try harder, and have fun. The parents done great job to follow my advice and we had fun games for all including referee. I think the clubs and coaches should frequently remind parents for respectful and supportive conduct toward referee and kids in the games.

After receiving Political Asylum, we had the opportunity to apply for residency and citizenship, which motivated us to develop a long-term plan for the family's future in America. Bahar's employment was our next big task. She would make a great employee for any organization, but fortunately, Computing Services had an opening position for a programmer in Administration Computing. Bahar applied for the position, and after two interviews, she was hired with a salary of $14,000 annually. The great thing was, we both were working in the same building, in two branches of the same department, even Department of the Computer Science was in this building. With both of us working and with two incomes, plus my teaching income, we finally were able to move out of our student-housing apartment into a bigger rented home. We rented a duplex with a private yard. After five years of struggle, scarify, and hard work we got closer than ever to build strong foundation for our family's future in generous and beautiful America. After moving to a bigger rental house, we bought a little black kitten named him Casie. Casie became most important part of the family and the next 17 years, he was best friend of all of us.

When Sheila was in third grade, she participated in her school's spelling bee and correctly spelled many difficult words. She reached the final five, then final three, before missing a word. Her advancement within just a few years — from not knowing English — was an indication of a bright future for her education.

The next two years we were busy with both of us working and involved in the girls' sports and school activities. In addition to her regular job, Bahar got involved in the development of some major administrative software such as advising, grading, and course scheduling for the university.

I continued with my team in the innovative work in the development of computer simulations and case studies for many departments. Sadly, Dr. Vebrougie left and went to work for a university in California. It was his vision and support that created one of the first instructional computer products in the country, and we missed his visionary leadership.

My department had no shortage of opportunities in the rapid-growing computer technology industry. In 1980s, interactive online computer simulation and case study for teaching and learning was new in higher education. My team at Ball State University were early pioneer in this field. Two early simulation software programs I developed with Dr. Pichtel, from Natural Resources, were Water and Air Pollutions software. These were used extensively for years as teaching and learning tools in the Natural Resources Department and were selected and included in the book as the first group of computer simulation software in the country by Iowa State University. We sold a few copies of the two developed simulation software to other universities. In addition of my work in Academic Computing, I had taught Basic, Fortran, COBOL, and Assembler2 for Computer Science Department.

Dr. Herb Stahlke, from the English Department, was selected as the new Director of Academic Computing. His background in teaching was a great asset and my future work in computer science and education. Dr. Stahlke encouraged the group by extending academic software development and services to include graphics, artificial intelligence systems, and virtual reality.

From 1981 to 1986, Bahar and I focused on saving enough money to build a house. Fortunately, land and houses were less expensive in Muncie than in other parts of the country. In 1986, we bought a half-acre lot in a new, upcoming subdivision called

Farmington, which was only ten minutes from the university campus. Seven years after

arriving in America, we accomplished the great American dream to build our own

home.

We continued to save money and purchased a wooded lot, one street down from

our house. The new land was an investment or could be a perfect place for building a

future house in the wooded area.

From 1986 and going forward, my focus shifted to the development of Expert System, a

branch of Artificial Intelligence (AI). Our team developed the first AI Expert System,

which was an assistance system on the mainframe to answer users' computer questions,

and our team attended many national and international conferences as presenters or

participants.

In 1988, I received a $10,000 grant from the Provost Office to evaluate the use of

Virtual Reality (VR) in education, which was a new area nationally — not many had

heard of this technology. I bought a Virtual Reality glass from Active Vision for $1,200;

the VR glass operated by battery. I also bought a Space Bar to move items in the

computer and used programming language C++ for development of virtual reality

applications. It was a fun, learning project, and many faculty members and students

came to my office to see demonstrations of virtual reality programs. Our work in simulation, Virtual Reality, and Artificial Intelligence were among the early work in

these areas at higher education institutions around the country.

For the next few years, I worked on major projects, including two of the most

widely used Artificial Intelligence systems: Surgical Expert System for the School of

Nursing, with Dr. Kay Hodson and two other faculty members; and Remediation of

Chemical Spill, with Dr. Pichtel from Department of Natural Resources. These two early

AI systems in education were known nationally and took about five years to develop —

each had over 1,500 rules.

The two AI systems and their contributions in teaching and learning were

presented and published in many national and international conferences and journals.

All the developed case studies, simulations, and intelligent systems were a major part of

online, hands-on learning and lab assignments of many departments. In those early

days, we did not have any of today's development tools — writing extensive code was

required for developing all programming and graphics.

For the Surgical Expert System, I drew, by hand, hundreds of charts showing

how they are related to each other, like a web. I used OPS5 programming language to

transfer knowledge of experts to a computer environment, and to establish meaningful

relationships in the knowledge base. Today, IBM Watson is a gigantic sample of Expert

System.

197

Meanwhile, the president of the university, Dr. John Worthen, was a great supporter of instructional computing in the education. With his and Dr. Kramer's encouragement, Academic Computing arranged annual fairs for the university to display and present all the developed software for classrooms and labs. All the faculty members involved in the development presented their software, and the majority of the university's faculty and staff visited the fair. The main purpose of these fairs was to encourage other faculty members to use computer applications in teaching and learning, and they were a great success. Dr. Worthen attended each of these annual events with interest. He spent a great deal of time experimenting with most of the developed software and asked in detail the development processes and collaborative work of faculty and my team members. He appreciated the good work of all involved and encouraged me to extend our services in the development of the educational software in the university.

In summer 1990, Bahar, Sheila, Shadi and I traveled to Sweden to visit my brothers and their family. After 12 years, we appreciated having the chance to see our family members, and it was very special for Sheila and Shadi to get to know members of their family other than Bahar and me. We enjoyed the three weeks with our family in the Uppsala and Stockholm Sweden and returned with a great deal of memories.

In November 1990, we were fortunate that my mother came to visit us when we were living in Muncie. It was a great chance for all of us to see her for the last time. She spoiled us with many unique Persian dishes. Grandchildren enjoyed her company and loved receiving full attention and kind remarks from their grandmother. She was so proud of all four us that endured the challenges of a new country and created a new life with bright future for the family. After a month, she left for Sweden then from there to Iran. My mother died in the age of 78, about 20 years after my father's death.

In fall 1990, I started my doctoral program in Education with Cognate in Computer Science. The plan was during the day, I carry my assignments as university employee, and taking night classes over the next four years to accomplish my course work requirement. It was a tough four years with full time daily responsibilities and daughters who were active in sport and were getting close to finish high schools. As usual Bahar carried most of the load to give me enough time to go to classes, study and complete assignments. My doctoral assignments, projects, and papers were based on how we merged computer and learning, how online education would change the future, and how to convert learning/teaching models to computer intelligent systems. In the grandparent's day at school, Bahar and I told our daughters we'd come to school and each be their grandparent for that day. Both girls, especially Shadi, were not happy with this alternative.

The summer of 1991, Bahar's mother made plans to visit us in America. The news of her visit brought excitement and joy for all particularly for the children. Sheila and Shadi barely remembered their grandparents, but they used their imagination in describing their love and memories. America did not have embassy in Iran, and she had to go to the American Embassy in Cyprus to apply for a visa. Grandma was old and barely knew English, we made decision that I go to Cyprus to help her with Visa and travel to America. I arrived in Cyprus a day ahead and met her at the airport. We both were so happy to see each other after so many years, and we both had so many things to talk and to share. We stayed at a hotel on the beach of the Mediterranean Sea, where the daily temperature could reach 110 degrees. She enjoyed to seat at the balcony of the hotel to watch all the activities in the shore and tourists in the street. In the afternoon, I change to swimming suite and went to shore for swimming. When I jumped in the water and looked around, I saw many nude tourists who were swimming and were laying down on the sands. It was embarrassing situation if Grandma saw me in the middle of the naked swimmers. I rushed back to hotel, she asked, "why you came back so soon." I said, "It was too crowded, and weather was too hot."

Early in the next morning, we went to US Embassy. When we arrived, there were already more than a hundred people almost all from Iran made a line, which stretched down the dusty street in the front of the American Embassy. There was no place to sit and no cover to shelter from the blazing sun.

At around 8:00 a.m., a young man from the embassy came out to ask if there was an American in the waiting crowed who could speak Farsi. I raised my hand and he asked for my passport and my occupation. He then asked me to help the embassy as a translator for that day, explaining that their regular translator was sick. I told him my mother-in-law was with me and asked if she could come with me into the embassy. Bahar's mother, Sedigheh came with me into the air-conditioned room and was offered a Pepsi to drink. She also was the first one to receive a visa to America that day. I spent the entire day helping the embassy to interview about 100 applicants for visas to America. I could see the nervousness and anxiety in the face of the applicants. Their ultimate wish and goal was to be granted travel visa to America. To convince the Ambassador, some cried, and some provided the most bizarre explanations in Farsi, which I had to rephrase it to make sense in English. Ambassador was very smart, at some point asked, "Please translate what they said, and don't change it." I said, "will do my best."

After four days in Cypress, we flew to Indianapolis, where Bahar and grandchildren were waiting for her. It was an emotional and tearful gathering at airport. The hugging and kissing were continued for a long time. The grandma sat between two grandchildren and most of the way I heard their voices and laugh. I heard she was telling the grandchildren "you are not in my arm every day, but you are in my mind and my heart every moment of my life." Sedigheh was proud to see our family's initial successes in America, and the grandchildren's progress in education. She enjoyed our new house and daily short walk in the neighborhood. She loved the clean street with colorful houses and beautiful yards with flowers and lawn. She made our favorite Persian foods and fed children as much as possible. She loved the American style life, freedom to talk, to wear what you wish, and to go anywhere you want. She enjoyed seeing smiling faces in the neighborhood, restaurants, and mall. She knew French and a little English, but without hesitation could start conversations with strangers. She stayed a month with us and brought a new energy and happiness to our family to continue our rebuilding new life in the new country. Being with grandma was so joyful for Sheila and Shadi that we wish they have had an adapted grandparent.

Bahar and I asked a good friend and colleague Lavada to be with the kids during grandparent's day at school. We thought this might be a one-time happening, but Lavada and her husband George became wonderful permanent adopted grandparents. Sheila and Shadi loved them and they treated the two adopted grand children with love and deep affection.

When George passed away a few years ago, Bahar, Shadi, and I traveled from Seattle and L.A. to be with Lavada at George's funeral. Recently Lavada took the long trip from Indiana to Seattle to be with us for a week. I remember, before knowing Lavada and George, our older daughter frequently asked us "In case something happens to you two, what we do? We don't know anybody in America?" After Lavada and George, she never repeated that question.

In 1992, my mother Layla travelled from Iran to Sweden to see my brothers. Fortunately, she was able to get visa and came to America to see us. The news of her trip was exciting for all four of us, especially for the children to see their other grandmother. We drove to Chicago Airport to meet her upon arrival to America. It was a gift to have her for a few weeks with us, we knew this might be the last time we could see her. She sat in the back seat with Sheila and Shadi, they talked mixed of English and Farsi. Children had a great time with their grandmother, and she made so many delicious dishes of Persian foods for us. She enjoyed a daily short walk around neighborhood and was impressed with beautiful yards and houses. It was a blessing in the last two years the children could see both grandmothers.

In 1992, we sold our first house after our larger house built on the wooded lot was finished. The new house gave the girls plenty of room to play, and kept us busy tending the yard, flowers, shrubs and big trees. It was our home for fifteen years, long after Sheila and Shadi left for college.

In addition to moving into our new home that year, 1992 was big year for us for another reason: our family became eligible for citizenship. That summer, all four of us appeared at the Indianapolis Courthouse and became US citizens. It was an emotional day for all four of us, half of our heart and mind were full of love and memories of Iran, and the other half was bursting rapidly with love and memories of our new country, America. We were honored to become citizens of this great country that accepted us, provided us opportunities to receive the best education, to work in great university, to succeed in life, and to be free. After the citizenship ceremony, we returned to the university, where friends and colleagues gathered for a major party for Bahar and me. At the end of party, they gave us American flag, which is with us after all these years. We always remember their kind words and generous welcome to the new country as citizen. That evening, adopted grandparent, Lavada and George came to see us, they brought for us an apple pie, a baseball, and small Chevy car as the symbols of our new country. We always remember their great hearts and kindness.

After four years, I completed my class work by 1994, and began work on my dissertation with the topic, "Future of Online Education" — which may have been one of the first in this new field in the country. For a year, I worked hard with my advisors on the design and development of the research activities. In addition to collecting statewide data from the state's higher education institutions, I spent more than six months in our campus library and in libraries of neighboring universities to collect information for the dissertation.

In 1996, I completed my dissertation, and, after two tries, the dissertation was accepted by my doctoral committee and the graduate office of the university. In May 1996, I received my doctoral degree at a campus-wide ceremony.

Higher education has been a major part of my life. I was fortunate to study in colleges four times, in four decades, for four different degrees. I have always loved math, and my hope is to one day to get a fifth degree, in Mathematics, from the University of Washington.

I always encourage my grandchildren to give their best in education. My youngest grandchild, Aaron, once told me that someday he will complete five degrees to beat me.

15

Exclusion, Difficult Years and Scholarly Work

In 1996, Ball State University hired a dean from one of its colleges to run

Information Technology and oversee three departments, Computing Services, Teleplex,

and Library, with about 400 staff members. The new dean transferred Dr. Stahlke back

to the English Department and brought in someone from Home Economics to run

Academic Computing. She had little or no knowledge about computer programming,

software development, graphics, databases, development methods, and intelligent

systems, yet wanted to change most of the current processes without seeking any input

from me or my group members.

My group had developed many interactive hands-on software programs that were

being used by the new head of Information Technology when he was the dean of the

college. He had personally, and in writing, expressed his appreciation for the great

expertise and contributions my team and I provided to his previous college. When I

explained to the new leader in Academic Computing that we were going in the wrong

direction, I was removed from all my assignments and was asked to focus only on

teaching and writing papers. To show up from 8:00 to 5:00 and stay in my office. The

lady from Home Economic who was appointed to lead my team was the dean's lady friend and they married later.

Over the next five years, all my team members were transferred to different groups with new assignments. Our great teamwork and services to the university were dismantled.

At the time, I was depressed and unhappy with my job, but now I can look back positively and say it may have been a blessing for me to have the time to do more scholarly works. I spent six months writing a textbook, *Operating Systems,* which was published by University Publications. I used the text book in my computer science class, and the book also was used by a few other faculties as part of their class assignments. The whole idea of online education as a new method of providing learning opportunities to vast new learners, and the demand for this method of education, was growing exponentially. The online learners were adults who wanted an education that could help them in real-life situations.

My dissertation, one of the first few in this area, had become well-received, nationally and internationally. Many researchers and doctoral students asked permission to use my dissertation in their research. I was invited to serve on doctoral committees and to referee for journals, and the National Science Foundation asked me to review some of their grant applications. Part of my dissertation was published in Chinese, Hebrew, and Arabic.

When I saw so much demand for new knowledge in this field, I initiated two other national researches with focus on the pedagogy and andragogy in online education. Dr. McHelinny, my doctoral advisor, joined me in these two national researches. We sent questionnaires to universities around the country, collected data, developed reports, and published the results in national journals. I also created a Research Website, which had my dissertation, broken into three sections, my second and third research reports, and links to other useful and related sites. For the next 10 years, the website was used by teachers, students, doctoral candidates, universities, and online education providers, nationally and internationally. Two years after my retirement, Ball State University changed its servers and applications to new platforms, and my research website disappeared.

I still did not have any defined assignment in the department. It was hard to keep myself busy for 8 hours every day in a closed door in my office. I was looking for a new opportunity that could fill the daily hours in the office and mentally challenges me. Meanwhile, Columbia University announced a plan to write a book with focus on the future. To select writers around the world for the book, Columbia accepted a few pages of draft chapters from writers. I prepared and sent a few pages of my idea for a chapter about "Forces of Changes: Knowledge Society and Adults Learners." The subject was new and not many written publications were available about these two topics.

Many scholars from around the world participated in this prestigious opportunity. I was one of the twenty-one selected. Most were from universities in United States, with a few from other countries. I was excited to be included in this rewarding initiative. During the next six months, I wrote a few drafts and a final copy. In 2000, the book, *Case Studies on Information Technology in Higher Education: Implications for Policy and Practice*, was published by Idea Group Publishing Company and was distributed worldwide. The book was on the best sellers list for a year. I received many questions and comments from readers all over the world. I also received a letter from Idea Publishing Company offering me full support to write a book about Knowledge Society, which was a new and futuristic subject. I could not accept the offer, because after five years, unexpectedly, I received a major assignment and a promotion to work with the new Vice president of the Information Technology.

For the next twelve years, my book chapter was available on the Amazon website, with all proceeds going to Columbia University. A summary of my research and work in online and distance education was printed at the first page of the annual European Conference in education, and my work in Knowledge Society was mentioned in the annual meeting of United Nation, New York.

The five years of isolation from daily services and contributions were painful. There were a few new opportunities for leadership in my group, for which I applied, but I was not selected. I always respected the decisions, but because of my superior qualifications, co-workers began to speculate that I was not offered jobs because of my accent, and uncompromised work ethics — I would not play politics. The situations never discouraged me or diminished my deep appreciation for the university. In university, if you are not tenured, you have an annual contract and could be terminated at the time of renewing the annual contract. I was not tenured and during those five years, and I was told by the leader of the department that the university might not renew my contract. Every summer, Bahar and I were worried about my contract not being renewed.

In 1997, I made an appointment with Dr. Worthen, the President of the university. He knew me from conducting the annual educational fairs and for developing innovative learning computer applications for the university. In addition, he and I had played on a tennis team twice a week at the YMCA. I told him about termination of my contract, and he told me do not worry — that he knew my work and my character, and that so many people spoke highly about me. He assured me that I would be a member of the university for as long as he was there. He offered to move me to another department, still I am not sure why I said "NO" to him.

Meanwhile, Bahar was doing such a great job, she was promoted to a leadership position. She led a team of five employees in the development of administrative software to assist in Admissions, Advising, Course Scheduling, Course Requests, Grades, and Graduation.

Even though we loved the university and Muncie was our home, Bahar and I ultimately made the decision to apply for jobs in other universities. I was invited to interview for positions of dean or vice president of Information Technology by a few universities. At Southern Connecticut University, I was one of the two finalists. When I met with the president of the university and gave my presentation, he was so excited, he asked my permission to copy all pages and slides of my presentation. He said it was exactly the design and direction Information Technology was supposed to follow.

After meeting with the committee, the chair took me for a tour and showed me where I should rent or buy home. I was over 90 percent sure that I would get the job and was happy to be in New Haven, home to Yale University. A few weeks later, I received a letter that the job was offered to the other candidate.

In another university in Illinois, I was one of the top two candidates again, and after two interviews the job was offered to the other candidate. I received a private note from the president of the university, indicating that I was his choice, but he could not convince the Board of Trustees and the Board selected the other candidate.

Despite the setbacks, I did not lose my belief that good work and knowledge would not be lost for long. I believed that America was the land of opportunity and I knew someday I would be recognized and given the right opportunity.

During this time, I discovered a new passion: Martial Arts. I had worked more than

twelve years in the Iranian forces dealing with criminals. Over 98 percent of the people

in our beautiful America are good and decent people, but 1 to 2 percent are unfit and

criminals that are far more than any society, and parents, should have to deal with.

From experience, I believe it is parents' responsibility to prepare children with basic

knowledge in how to deal with unexpected, dangerous situations, and if possible, to

learn the basics of self-defense. When Sheila was eleven, and Shadi was only eight, I

registered them in Tae-Kwon-Do at Muncie's YMCA. Two wonderful police officers,

Mr. Walker, a third-degree black belt, and world-champion Mr. Sheridan, a fifth-degree

black belt, were their Sensei. Both children were good athletes and were learning and

advancing rapidly. I continued my boxing practices with a punching bag at home, and I

had some knowledge of Judo from my military academy training.

After the children's first year in martial art classes, I signed up to join them. Both

Sheila and Shadi already had blue belts and in the Do Jo they were senior to me.

Sometimes they made jokes about the situation and ordered me around in the Do Jo.

After four years, Sheila and Shadi received their black belts. They both wanted to

pursue another sport, and Bahar and I encouraged them to sign up for tennis at the

YMCA. I continued Martial Arts for the next few years and received my first- and second-degree black belts. I taught some classes and my focused changed to Martial

Arts training. The children's tennis activities were the main reason we met our friends

for life (Pat and Rebecca Looney) that their children were tennis players too.

The Computer Science department had a visiting professor from China, who was

a master in Tai Chi Chuan. In addition to teaching Computer Science, he conducted Tai

Chi classes, which I joined and learned some basics. A year later, we had a young

woman Sensei who was fifth-degree black belt and a great Tai Chi instructor. Bahar and

I continued learning Tai Chi by participating in her classes, and eventually, we became

very good teachers in this art. We conducted many classes in Tai Chi, mostly

volunteering our time, for universities, hospitals, churches, and YMCAs. The university

developed a DVD from our Tai Chi Chuan class and placed it in the library for students,

faculty, and community access.

Learning the basics of safety and self-defense can be lifesaving. With the university

students' safety in mind, the Wellness Department asked me to teach self-defense

classes to students and faculty.

Over the next few years, with the help of Sheila and Shadi, we conducted self-defense

classes for the Wellness Department and girls' dorms at Ball State University. Sheila and

Shadi were fourteen and eleven at the time; teaching at the university was a great

experience for both. The three of us wrote a paper about self-defense and criminals, which even after 25 years, is still helpful, as I have shared it with self-defense

participants and friends.

16

Great Assignments,

Great Services to City Schools and Great Rewards

When Bahar and I came to the United States, the American culture was new to us. We were a family of four without any relatives in this large country. We believed that education was key for our small family's prosperity and survival in this great society, and when children became old enough, and we became more settled in our careers, focused fully on the children's education.

Sheila was one of the top students in her high school. She was also popular and a good athlete. She was elected homecoming queen and played on the state-champion varsity tennis team for three years. She studied pre-med, biology, and chemistry earned all "A"s and only one B as an undergraduate. She achieved a high score on the MCAT and was pre-accepted into Indiana University's Medical School.

Sheila met a fine young man, Wade, while in medical school, and while completing their residency programs at Medical Hospital of University of Minnesota, they bought their first house and married. Friends and relatives of both families attended their wedding, including my three brothers from Sweden. We are blessed to have three grandchildren, Nathan, Clare, and Aaron. Bahar and I traveled to Minneapolis to be part of their lives from beginning on the first day they were born, and ultimately

followed them to the suburb of Seattle, Washington.

Shadi also excelled in education and tennis. She was state-ranked tennis player, a

number-one single for her school for three years and finished third in state

championship. After her freshman year in high school, she transferred to Burris

Academy, a high school in partnership with Ball State University. From a young age,

Shadi's wish was to study in a university far away from Indiana, to gain new social and

life experiences. It did not quite work out that way. After graduation from Burris, she

enrolled in political science at Ball State University, and then continued to complete the

graduate program at Ball State. She was part of University Tennis team and competed

in many tournaments but had wrist injury that forced her to quit tennis after first year.

She passed the LSATs and chose New England School of Law at Boston, without

hesitation. Three years later, Shadi graduated from law school and was hired by a

company in Minneapolis, which gave her the opportunity to live near Sheila. She

passed the Minnesota bar exam and stayed with company for two years, until a position

was offered to her by an international consulting firm at Los Angles.

She moved to Los Angeles and traveled around the country to work with other

employees in providing consultations for client-companies and is now an Executive

Director in the Company. Shadi has a great future in the leadership and capable to run a major corporation. Shadi is a wonderful aunt for her niece and nephews. They see her as a friend and great supporter.

In the 1990s, one of the most discussed issues in the computer industry was the change of date at the beginning of a new century — Y2K. The concern was that the dates in the new century would cripple all different phases of education, business, and government dependent on computer systems and applications for daily operations. Ball State University was no exception. The university's daily business, educational activities and plan, communications were dependent on over thousands of computer applications used in admissions, advising, student course scheduling and registration, student grade records, graduation, bursar, and so forth.

Bahar was selected to lead the Year 2000 conversion project. The project took more than three years and included the participation of many project managers and programmers from almost every department at Ball State. Bahar worked tirelessly with the contributors, developed detailed action plans and schedules, and kept track of the outcomes. She oversaw changes, conversions, tests, and the implementation of modifications that affected more than a thousand programs to be compatible with the year 2000.

The three years of Bahar's hard work resulted in a smooth transition to year 2000 without any halt in operations of the university. Her great contributions were appreciated by her department and by the many university communities that depended on computer systems to conduct daily operations and activities.

In 2002, the dean of Information Technology retired, and the university hired Dr. O'Neal Smitherman as Vice President of Information technology. I was one of two internal candidates qualified for the position of the Director in my department, but in the final evaluation with the committee, the other candidate was offered the job. The matter of selection reached to our new vice president and he made the decision to move me to the Administration Building and promoted me as his Special Assistant. This was a great promotion and opportunity for me to contribute in a much different capacity to the university.

I had been excluded from many major projects the previous five years, and I saw this as a major break in my career before retirement. Mentally, I was exhausted and in some cases I lost my sharpness with all the new changes in the technology and had to work harder to catch up with the lost time. The core of my new assignment was my ability in planning, arranging campus wide team, and generate expected outcomes for the campus wide and community projects. I was confidence that I will do a great job in the new assignment. At my first meeting with the vice president, he explained how I could help him with special campus wide projects. I told him to remember someday in the future, you would tell me, "Bringing me to leadership was the best decision you made at the University." He remembered this statement a few years later when he accepted a new assignment in Alabama. In our last meeting, he repeated my full statement and told me I was 100 percent right.

My office was in the Administration Building, along with my friend Phil Repp, associate vice president, a talented web, graphics, and presentation designer, and the office manager. My assignment always required to assemble a variety of talents from multiple colleges and departments.

One morning, the vice president called me into his office to discuss a project – funded by about $800,000.00 grant from Congress. Over the past six months, another group at the university had been working on it, but without much progress. I was given full responsibility to lead the planning and execution of the project, manage team's assignments, and report of the positive outcomes. The project, called Digital Middletown Project (DMP), was to use a new long-distance wireless technology, WiMAX, to connect a few elementary schools around the city, and provide them with high bandwidth wireless connections, all the classroom technology, online content, training and support services. We would research the capabilities of long-distance wireless technology to access learning resources, using computer and online contents in daily learning activities, measure the educational advancement of the students, and report results to Congress. In addition, the project was supposed to connect about 15 houses with the WiMAX technology to evaluate entertainment possibilities of this new long-distance wireless technology. Schools around Muncie and almost everywhere were struggling to provide classroom technologies for teachers and students. I saw this grant and partnership with major technology companies could be a great opportunity to help a few schools with the best available classroom technologies. The success of the project also could be a message for those who excluded me from any assignments in the last five years.

I formed my research and development team, which included university faculty and staff from various departments (Information Technology, Education, Psychology, and Telecommunications), as well as some top graduate and undergraduate students. With the university talent in place, we approached several corporations in the technology and communications industry and invited them to join the project. A few members of the team and I traveled three times to Washington DC to meet with Department of Education, Department of Energy, and partner Digital Bridge Company. We also travelled to California to meet and have presentation with technology partners, Alvarion, Intel, Google, Proxim, Cisco, and Xirrus.

After interviews and discussions with a few schools, we selected three elementary schools that were 7, 4, and half a mile away from campus to participate in this unique study. One of the selected schools was the one that my daughters attended in the early ages and I knew the principal of the school. we also selected fifteen homes

from neighborhoods close buy to be part of the research activities.

The technology in the three participating schools and the fifteen homes was ready to go,

thanks to products donated by our generous corporate partners: Alvarion and Proxim

donated WiMAX long distance point to point connections; multiple Cisco Wi-Fi,

donated by Cisco; Gateway donated laptops to the teachers, and also 50 laptops to each

school, along with chargers and moving carts; Xirrus donated needed technology to

create online access in the Yorktown Library; and Discovery Company gave each school

full access to Discovery Educational resources, United Streaming, for online teaching

and learning. Digital Bridge was a major partner to facilitate partnerships with all the

corporate partners. From other various donors, schools also received video

conferencing equipment, video cameras, and display screens in the classrooms. Vice

President Dr. Smitherman, Dr. Yoden, Dr. Jones from Department of

Telecommunication, and Mr. Kelly Dunne from Digital Bridge were major part of

communications and negotiations with partner technology companies around the

country. Digital Middletown Project's partner schools provided six teachers, two from

each participating school, with basic training in using laptop computers, accessing

online applications, problem solving, collecting data, and technology-based

teaching/learning methodology. Our technology, research, and GIS members of the team had done amazing jobs to design, implement, and evaluate this unique and difficult project. For the mapping the strength of the wireless signals and develop a 3-D design of the network, with the help of the two talented members (Paul Shanayda and Brian Hatton), we contacted the HNET-BALTIC in the Liutvenia, which had the most advance technology software in this area. The company accepted our partnership invitation and free of the charge donated its development software to the project. In addition, its Vice President came to campus for a few days training of the DMP network team members. I went twice a week to each school to talk with principals and teachers to learn about the activities and progresses. The schools were beyond of description appreciative and happy for this great opportunity. I felt the most satisfaction in my life when I sat in the classrooms and observed the teachers' passionate teaching and students' eager faces to watch contents on the display screen and to work with computers. I received some hand-written letters from students (third and fourth grades) that simply thanked me to give them computer and helped them to learn better. The joy of those memories and reading those wonderful letters still makes my heart happy.

The three-year project was a huge success and received national-level exposure. The Digital Middletown Project accomplished a great deal for the university, the corporate partners, and the schools, as well as for the technology industry. With extensive research and evaluation, the teams reported positive contributions of the technology in teaching, learning, and entertainment. The following is the design of the

DMP network to those three schools, Library, and homes.

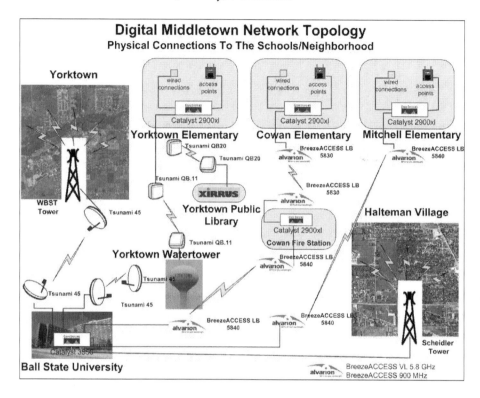

School, Library, Homes Network, DMP Project

In 2006, the university leaders met with top executives from the corporate

partners at Ball State University to discuss the project results and the university's role

moving forward. The corporate executives noted how in demand our experience and

services were in wireless research, design, and development. They recommended to Dr.

Gora, President of the university that Ball State developed a for profit business company to offer our expertise in this new field. Dr. Smitherman and I were designated to initiate the new company, which would reside in the University Incubator.

After months of long, hard work by many experts in the university, we designed and developed Afterimage GIS Company to offer wireless mapping and services nationally. Contributions of the Dr. Larry Cox, Director of the Entrepreneur Department was a great asset to design the business model of the new company and its operational plan. For the first year with help of Paul and Brian, I led the operation and activities of this new company. Three of us also successfully negotiated our first big contract, for both the first year, and a renewal for the second year with the Digital Bridge Company in the Washington DC.

A year later, two of our team members (Paul and Brian) resigned from the university, registered Afterimage GIS as an LLC with Indiana Business Bureau, and became president and vice president of Afterimage, as well as having major ownership of the company. Because of bad advisement of person in charge of the developing spin off company, the university rejected the proposal offered for the percentage of profit they would receive from Afterimage. I continued as General Counsel to Afterimage GIS, and after my retirement from the university, I was offered 9% of the company's shares and its annual profits — the company I helped develop and establish. To date, I have not received a single payment from the company, but I am sure someday if I need financial help my friends Paul and Brian will be there for me, as I was for them at Ball State University and the development of the company.

My role in advancing online learning technology to all levels of education and working with K-12 schools in a few major projects, is my proudest contributions during my career at Ball State University. The success and accomplishments of the DMP project was a validation of my ability to contribute and proved the five years unfair exclusion was unjustified. I was promoted to Assistant Vice President of the university. The success of the DMP project and to continue future research, the university developed a new department, Office of Wireless Research and Mapping (OWRM) and appointed me as the first director of this new department. This assignment was in addition to the job I maintained as Assistant to Vice President of Information Technology. My new assignment provided me more opportunities to help university and to attract new technology partners to the university. In addition of Dr. Smitherman, Dr. Jo Ann Gora, the President of the university was a great supporter of the DMP, and her positive comments were appreciated greatly.

With President Gora and Dr. Smitherman, Mr. Repp

The success of Digital Middletown Project continued to open doors in the form of

lease agreements for our technology and grants for research and development. I was

able to negotiate with and convince the branch of the Governor's Office that provided

oversight to spectrum technology in Indiana (IHETS) to transfer three 802.16 long

distance wireless, or point-to-point network connectivity, from Indiana University to

Ball State University for research. I also led the negotiations for a 15-year lease of these

three spectrums to Digital Bridge Company, which brought in $100,000 annually to Ball

State University. These new accomplishments were appreciated by the President and

Vice President of the university in many sessions and in the form of salary raise. When I looked back to the last 60 years, I could not believe how a boy from small town in Iran, could survive all those challenges in the life and after 40 years of hard work still impatiently waiting for the next big challenge. Fortunately, next big challenge arrived on time and I was called to lead a new campus and community wide grant project that was a nationally important one.

In 2005, The Department of Energy awarded us a $250,000.00 research grant to identify the strengths and weaknesses in teaching and learning methods applied to science and math in the schools. I was appointed by the university to lead this nationally significant and needed project. I assembled a team of three researchers from Teachers College; a development team from Computer Science and Art; selected five teachers in biology, math, physics, and chemistry from local elementary and high schools; and a professional multimedia and game development company, based in Indianapolis. After extensive literature review and evaluations, the assembled team concluded that the current model of learning using only speech, books, and blackboards did not interest our school students, when they were spending a great deal of time playing online interactive games and accessing materials online. The review revealed that students in middle school were at the most crucial stage to learn the basics of math and science. Adding hands-on, game-based learning opportunities in the basics of science and math could help the team to measure the effectiveness of this method of learning.

The team developed eight interactive multimedia games as learning tools to aid in teaching physics, chemistry, biology, and math. The results were evaluated in countless research methods, with more than 350 middle school participants.

Once again, the talents of Ball State University delivered another successful project. The results of the study and the potential of the new learning technology was shared at national and local conferences and appeared in multiple publications and journals. The team believed that with the gained experiences in development and research, it is crucial to establish a development company to continue development of short hands on games in science and math. To acquire funding for the development of a database with more than 500 short games — 125 games in each of four subjects — we submitted proposals to Gates Foundation, Department of Education, and Department of Energy. We requested $5,000,000 to establish a new company to develop online games for teaching and learning math and science. The design of the company, and development process were such a unique one that was called "Holy Grail Model."

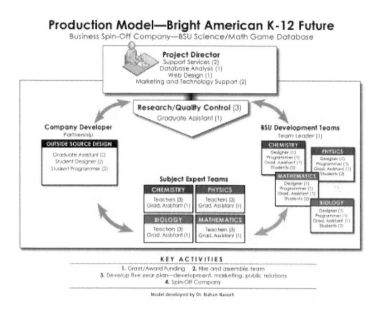

Production Model—Bright American K-12 Future
Business Spin-Off Company—BSU Science/Math Game Database

New Company--Production Design, Solve Math Science Problems

My argument in the proposal to Department of Education, Energy, and Gates

Foundation was, we have about 2,500,000 home schooling students, and each family

spent about $700.00 annually for home schooling materials. If we charge only $20.00 for

the home-schooling students to access all year the database of the science and math,

then the income only from home schooling students would be about $50 million.

In addition of home schooling, there would be a bigger income from charging

only $50 annually to public and private schools for teachers and students to access the

database. Most of the science and math concepts are international and could be a good market internationally for the accessing the database. The initial cost would be around $5,000,000.00, and the continued annual cost of the operations of the new company would be about $3,000,000.00 annually. The contributions of the created game-based science and math database to K-12 students in the United State could be priceless. The Department of Education was impressed by the design of the company and arranged a conference call to discuss further actions. In the conference call, I quoted from the Chronicle of Higher Education in an article dated 10/16/2007: "Fifty years after Sputnik — USA is in another equally important race that will define our leadership. During the past two years, academic and business leaders have called for government to respond by increasing science spending on a scale comparable what it did after Sputnik. American Compete Act Law—August 2007."

The Department of Education in the conference call indicated that expectation was for Congress to approve the massive budget and that my project would be among the first to receive the seed money for development of a company to help increase the learning capabilities of our young people, from kindergarten through high school, in one of the weakest areas in our country's education system: math and science. Learning through online games that have been developed using state-of-the-art research and technology, can help our children reach their full learning potential and become better prepared to compete in a global market.

Each organization I approached praised our design of the science and math game development company and emphasized the great national need for this company to deliver the product, but none would commit to contribute funding the initial expenses. A major hurdle for the development and establishment of a company for our team's product was timing: I planned to retire the following year. I tried desperately, and without success, to obtain funding in the months I had left at Ball State.

In addition of Assistant to the Vice President duties, I continued to lead the Office of Wireless Research and Mapping and its staff members as Director until my retirement in July 2008.

Further recognition of our efforts was given to my boss and good friend. *CIO Magazine* selected Dr. O'Neal Smitherman as the 2006 CIO of the Year and published a wonderful long article about our Digital Middletown Project. The Project's outcomes, including creation of Research Center and Afterimage GIS, were key credentials for this prestigious award for Dr. Smitherman and the University.

17

Meeting President Obama

Every Tuesday evening and Saturday morning, I played tennis with a group of

faculty and the city's professionals at the Muncie YMCA indoor tennis center. In fall

2007, a Saturday morning, Bahar gave me ride to YMCA. When I entered the building, I

saw a few people in dark suits and ties in the hallway. The front desk told me Mr.

Obama, who was a candidate for president at the time, was in the gym on the treadmill.

I asked the guards if I could say hi and shake Mr. Obama's hand. The guard said yes, he

would be happy to talk with me.

I left my tennis bag at the front door and went inside the workout room. Mr. Obama

was reading a local newspaper while walking on the treadmill. The room was very

quiet, and a few people were exercising. I walked over next to him and said hi, and he

kindly stopped reading, turned his head, and responded by saying good morning. He

shook my hand. I welcomed him to Muncie, and he thanked me for my greeting

comment. I briefly explained that I was working on a major education project, which

was a very important "Science Literacy Project" for the future of science and math in

schools. Mr. Obama listened with deep attention, and I mentioned that if he became president, I would send him a grant proposal for creation of a company dedicated to the development of science and math games for middle and high school students.

In summer 2008, Bahar and I retired with emeritus status from Ball State University. As a family, we were fortunate to live in Muncie a good size city with great people and affordable housing. We blessed to be educated and worked in a wonderful higher education institution, Ball State University. All family members attended this quality university and received solid education for a successful professional carrier. Ball State University had about 20,000 students, and over 3,000 faculty and staff. It is medium size university, but somehow all faculty and staff knew each other and had a family environment feeling through the campus. Education is a great bridge for understanding, tolerance, and equality. University with educators and students is a perfect place for an immigrant family to feel welcome and be accepted without any reservation within community. We were fortunate to spend 30 years of our life in this environment and never ever felt our quality were measured by our accent or origin.

After city lost some of the General Motors auto factories and Ball Corporation, university became more vital for the city and its citizen. The campus is beautiful, easy to walk, and all can enjoy its landscape and buildings' architectural design. Happy faces and helpful hands will help you to learn and find what you wish to access or to know. When I needed to have a chance for acceptance to graduate program, even I was not ready at that moment, university trusted my words and life experiences, gave me opportunity to prove myself. When I needed a job and lost fate in finding job in open market, university offered me a job and trusted that I would deliver my assignments. When we had immigration and deportation problem, the campus community was ready to do whatever possible to help us with this unfair situation. When Bahar needed job, university hired her and presented her great opportunity to prove herself. When we became citizen of this great country, the generous and heartwarming receptions and celebrations by friends and colleague at our departments were from their great heart and pure kindness. When we retired from our beloved university, we felt empty, cold, and lonely. When we left Muncie to be with our grandchildren, we felt the same when we left Iran. Last 10 years, when somebody ask us where you are from, all family members tell, from Muncie Indiana. We are forever Hoosier and we are very proud of it. God bless Ball State University and Muncie.

After my retirement, I sent a letter to the President Obama, reminding him of our brief meeting at the YMCA and attaching the detailed proposal, including the designed model for the creation of a company to develop over 500 video games for K-12 students. The proposal was the result of years of work by a variety of experts to resolve issues in performance in science and math in the middle schools. The university team members including five K-12 teachers and professional game development partner believed it could be a great solution for the science and math problems in grades K-12 in the USA. After a month, I received a signed letter from President Obama thanking me for my proposal and indicating that he forwarded the proposal to the Department of Education. When you need funding for a project, never pass up an opportunity to ask for it. Unfortunately, I did not hear anything from the Department of Education and retiring and being away from an educational institution made it more difficult to seek a $5 million grant.

One of the great memories from university was, most of the colleague heard from me that I was from Texas. The related story is; during 1950s and 1960s most of the movies were cowboy's movies. We called those movies Texasy (from Texas) and we saw America as Texas and Cowboys. The last 38 years, when somebody in the classroom, campus, meetings, and public asked me where I was from, always said from Texas. I could see from their face, they were surprised by my response. Some did not ask more even though knew I am not from Texas, but some repeated their questions and added the word seriously at the end then I said from Persia. Most of them knew Persia is the old name of Iran and were satisfied with the answer and some wonder where was the Persia.

18

Retirement, Coaching, Teaching,

Effort to Develop a Sport Complex

The day Sheila gave birth to our first grandchild, Nathan, Bahar and I drove

twelve hours from Muncie to Minneapolis, hoping to be there for his arrival. We were

so fortunate to arrive at the hospital 30 minutes before he was born. He is a great gift to

our family, and as our first grandchild. Our beautiful granddaughter, Clare, was born

thirteen months later. She has made our life as sweet as possible.

In the first few years of their lives, Bahar and I made the drive to visit Nathan and Clare

in Minneapolis quite a few times each year. Three years after Clare was born, our

second grandson, wonderful Aaron, was born. Having these three fantastic

grandchildren are the treasures of our lives beyond imagination. It was because of them

that Bahar and I made the decision to retire in 2008 — to move from Muncie to

Minneapolis and later followed them to the suburb of Seattle to be closer to our

grandchildren. In the year before retirement, Bahar and I sold our house and rented a

small duplex in Muncie from a nice family. We moved to Minnesota and rented an

apartment in Minnetonka, ten miles from our grandchildren in Minneapolis.

Shortly after our move, our son-in-law, Wade, arranged a trip to take Nathan and me with him to New York. We enjoyed every minutes of our trip. We went to Yankees

Stadium to see baseball, Yankees against Minnesota Twins. We also watched the NY

Mets play the Philadelphia Phillies, then traveled by train to Philadelphia and watched

the Phillies and Twins game.

A few weeks later, Bahar and I took a trip to Sweden to visit my three brothers and their

families. After a week, we went to Germany for the wedding of Bahar's nephew. When

we returned to Minneapolis, the cold winter had arrived, and we wondered how we

could ever survive winter in Minneapolis. We began looking for a house to buy, but in

spring 2009, Sheila and Wade announced they were considering changing jobs and

moving to State of Washington. They both had successful interviews with a clinic and

hospital in the Puget Sound region.

Once again, Bahar and I moved and began looking for a new home. We settled in

a small, picturesque town on a peninsula, popular for vacationers, boaters, and retirees.

We bought a home about fifteen minutes away from our grandchildren, and within

walking distance of major stores, a grocery, restaurants, and a coffee shop. The

grandchildren love walking through woods and narrow roads to the nearby ice cream

shop.

Meanwhile, Shadi also changed jobs and moved from Minnesota to Los Angeles. Living

in Los Angles for the next eight years gave Bahar and me a great opportunity to travel a few times a year to be with Shadi — and to escape the rainy winter seasons in the Pacific Northwest. I coached Nathan and his first soccer team while in Minneapolis and continued for six years as coach or assistant coach for his team. To keep myself busy, I coached the Premier League at Soccer Club. No matter how much rain we have the soccer practice and game must goes on. My first game was with a team from Seattle at a field outside of the Seattle. It was rainy day and field was covered with patches of water. I told the other team's coach "Let's cancel the game," I saw the coach is laughing and told me "Are you new to this area?" I said "yes," he said, "we never cancel a game or practice because of the rain." I coached and assistant coached youth teams for the next 5 years. I was lucky to coach for one season my beautiful granddaughter Clare's soccer team, and for five seasons to coach my younger grandson Aaron's soccer team. The coaching of my grandchildren teams created so many heartwarming memories for me that I cherish them forever. Eventually, I was asked by Soccer Club as Executive Director of the Development to evaluate, and if possible, to develop a needed Soccer Complex for our town and the soccer club. I put together a development team that included the Director of Coaching; a professional business developer, who was the father of one of our players; and the President of the club. We met once a week to evaluate possibilities and share ideas for an action plan, which I prepared and maintained. I applied my experience and expertise in finding opportunities for potential grants, and researching development of an athletic complex, the process, and associated costs. We expanded our team to bring in the experience needed to advance our project, including finance, legal, and city administration.

In the first six months of our planning, I prepared comprehensive grant inquiries which I sent to The Gates Foundation, as well as the Milgard, Cheney, Russell foundations, and United State Youth Soccer Foundation. I prepared reports and delivered presentations, which explained in detail why an indoor/outdoor soccer complex with turf and lighted fields was needed, how the community would benefit, and how we would develop and pay for it. We selected potential building sites and designed a complex that would including a building to accommodate coaches, meetings, and classrooms. As an added benefit to the community, a walking trail would surround the complex for public use. To help with costs, fields and classrooms would be leased to other sports teams — lacrosse, baseball, football, and softball. We worked more than a year on the project and were confident we had enough interest and verbal agreements for seed money to seriously negotiate for the land.

The two great foundations Milgard and Cheney indicated their interest to help with complex development, and we had a successful presentation and meeting with the leadership of the Milgard foundation. The Milgard foundation indicated will help maximum of 25% of expenses and estimated expenses including land was about $10 million. Both great foundations indicated acquiring land was the platform for us to complete grant proposals to the foundations that required us to secure property before any grant would be awarded. The team had a few meetings and presentations with the officials of the City (mayor's team) about allocation of a future park to this project. Even I saw some interest and support, I could not convince the city for the allocation of the land.

We met with another group interested in an athletic complex for the community, PenMet. PenMet was in the charge of the Parks in the Peirce County, which had a strong presence in parks in the community and some funds for purchasing land. After six months meetings and negotiations, PenMet leadership verbally committed 20 acres in the Family Park for the development of the sport complex. I prepared a Memorandum of Understanding (MOU) for partnership, which included the commitment of the Soccer Club to develop the four turf and lighted fields in the 20 acres land.

We were all involved over year and half in the project, all volunteers, and team members spent a great deal of their own money in the process. It was a great relief that finally we are so close to secure the development land. After submitting our final MOU, I invited a team of experts from FieldTurf Company in Snohomish, Washington to visit the 20 acres land in the Family Park to provide us an accurate cost of development of the sport complex, which I would incorporate into my final grant proposals to Milgard and Cheney. A few days before FieldTurf team's visit, PenMet informed us that all partnership activities from their side were halted.

I lost my hope to secure land for sport complex, but I was told by the city that someday they hoped to develop the type of complex I had described. Meanwhile, the president of the Soccer Club resigned. He was a great person to work with, knew all the details of our activities, and had a great deal of knowledge for the development of the sport complex. His resignation and PenMet's pause were a major setback for the project. I provided all the details of the progresses, activities, presentations, and papers, and requested from the soccer club to be released from the project. I offered all my support and help if needed in their future activities.

My grandsons moved to Washington Premier Soccer Club, and I was approached by Washington Premier to help with grant proposals for their new projects, the addition of a new turf, lighted field, and purchase of a vacant school next to the complex. I provided the club with reports and data that I collected over the last two years, wrote a few grant inquiries to Milgard and Cheney foundations for the club, and offered to help more, if needed. I've also been asked by a friend and coach John Wedge to share my knowledge about grants possibilities with NW United, which is in the process of the development of a soccer complex. I shared some of my documents with the leader of the Skagit Soccer Complex development project.

In addition to the chance to remain involved in athletics, I enjoy helping and coaching the young people in our community and providing them an opportunity to play sports, which is critical to their physical, mental, and social development.

19

Painting, Writing Book, Trying to Satisfy Civic Duties

In retirement, I have spent a great deal of my time oil paintings. In the last ten years, I have finished over hundred paintings, some of which were donated to charities, some given to friends as gifts, and some passed on to my children and grandchildren. Sometimes, I was invited to Kindergarten or First grade Classroom to teach oil painting and paint a canvas with contributions of all the children in the classroom. It is so rewarding when I ask each child with my help to paint a portion of canvas. We all signed, and teacher took a group picture with the painted canvas. I have more than fifty oil paintings at home, and Bahar has a hard time to find places for them around the house and suggested we create a web site to sell the painting. I will continue my oil painting for the rest of my life. In addition of painting and exercise, writing the life story kept me busy.

I continue to teach in some capacity, including a few Karate classes at the local YMCA, and a few self-defense classes in Gig Harbor and Tacoma YMCAs. Bahar and I teach Tai Chi classes around the community, and we both exercises regularly at the YMCA. I still enjoy practicing my boxing with the punching bag.

Recently, a member of the city council resigned, and city announce the acceptance of application for this position. After long debate with family members, I forwarded my application including a short vita about my credential to the city. Eleven people were invited for an open to public interview. The process of interview and selection was somehow unusual. They asked each candidate to talk about their qualifications and accomplishments for only three minutes. In addition, in the three minutes, each candidate should also include his/her view about the five questions about city, which was submitted to them a few days before interview. I Knew I do not have any chance for this position. How in the world committee with three minutes presentation can make judgement which of the eleven candidates is the best to fit the job? It was clear that there was a candidate that selection committee was satisfied and already selected. In addition, for a person like me with accent it takes about 10 minutes the audience feel comfortable with the presentation. There were a few accounts of the interview, which worth to mention. One of the candidate told directly to committee, I am the best candidate for this job and should be selected, another candidate told to the committee they should select a women for the council, and finally at the end after selected candidate was announced, a councilmember mentioned that the reason we selected this young man is he already worked in the planning commission and know our process and work plan. This comment proved my initial thought that they knew who they wanted to select before even announcing the position. I had a brief talk with the selected young man, he was knowledgeable and could do a great job for the city, but I wondered why city wasted people times and played with their hope when committee already knew who was going to be selected for the job. I am sure there was a good reason beyond of my understanding and experience.

Finally, Bahar and I have bought an old house with a third of an acre of land. The greatest thing about this place is that Sheila and Wade bought the same size lot next to ours and the plan is to build a house next to us in a year. The second greatest thing is the house has a beautiful view of the Puget Sound and downtown. The house needs a major renovation. This area was growing beyond of the control and with new residents that are coming from around the country. Finding a good contractor to start immediately was an impossible task. We hired a contractor who quit after demolishing and framing the house. We hired a second contractor that started good but gave us a list of future costs far beyond of our allocated budget. Bahar and I made decision to lead the renovation ourselves. After 10 months of hassle we completed the renovation with almost twice of the cost that was estimated with the first contractor. The remodeled house has a lot of storage, so I will not be in trouble with Bahar to find storage for my oil paintings.

We appreciate the possibilities and challenges that life has offered to us so far. Now, at the seventy-three years old I am getting closer to the final chapter of my life. I am still looking forward impatiently, with great interest, for the next challenge in life. A few days ago, I saw a vacant position in the Planning Commission of the city. Bahar suggested I apply for the position, I submitted my application and waiting to hear from the city officials. This might be my next challenge.

As immigrants, Bahar and I are blessed to be in this beautiful country, to have had the opportunity to be educated with multiple degrees, served with honor, and retired. As immigrants, our two daughters worked hard in education, as physician and lawyer trying to serve this great country with highest quality. I am sure, our next generation, the grandchildren will accomplish highest level of the education, and will serve the society with excellence. The greatness of America is in its beautiful heart to accept, respect, and treasure immigrants in the last 230 years.

America's Beautiful Heart brighten my family's life and we are always grateful for its genericity and open heart. God Bless America.

The only thing I would like to ask is trying to understand immigrants, their battles in life, their accomplishments, and services to their new country. They are good people with dreams for better life, like your parents and grandparents when they immigrated. Be kind, understanding, and open minded with them.

A few samples of my Oil Paintings:

Made in the USA
Lexington, KY
31 October 2019

56348661R00138